O.G.

OBTAINING GREATNESS

How to Change Your Mindset So You
Can Change Your Life

O.G. - OBTAINING GREATNESS

How to change your mindset so you can change your life

ISBN 978-1-7330281-0-3 (paperback)

ISBN 978-1-7330281-1-0 (e-book)

ISBN 978-1-7330281-2-7 (audio book)

DEDICATION

To my mother, Glenda Buckley (Bae Bae). We've been through a lot together and there's never been a time you didn't support me. Thank you for showing me the meaning of unconditional love.

Foreword

When I first came to Saginaw, Michigan some 30 years ago I was amazed, disappointed and frustrated by the lack of leadership training opportunities for African-American men. I was born and raised in Flint, Michigan. I did not have a father figure in my home and I was the oldest brother of four. This forced me into making decisions without any type of guidance, for the most part, from a male figure which can be a land mine when you're growing up in tough environments. I witnessed a lot of that in Saginaw where there was little professional guidance from Black men who could help, support and lead those younger men coming into the professional ranks. Sure, there were the traditional religious figures, educators and even a few father figure coaches but few, if any, businessmen.

That inspired me. I was in rooms serving the community on boards of directors where many decisions were being made. There were no other black men or women, just me. The newspapers were full of pictures of young black men being arraigned on any number of felony charges. Certainly there had to be a vast number of black men who were not criminals, who were looking for opportunities with no one to provide guidance. That's when I started The Saginaw Valley African American Leadership Training Institute designed to expose Black men to the Great Lakes Bay Region business community and the business community to them. One of the first men who agreed to participate in that leadership class was the author ANDRE L. BUCKLEY, who was looking for jobs outside of the region since there were very few opportunities met his competencies and skill sets. During one of the sessions he met the

1

founders of Tri-Star Trust Bank and a professional relationship grew from that point forward between them and Andre. I watched Andre take that experience and develop this remarkable passion to ensure others would not have the same trials, tribulations, a lack of guidance, nor would they have to look outside of their own community to find great employment opportunities.

After reading this book I'm convinced Andre has achieved just that; a GPS system that will help anyone navigate through some of life's challenges and barriers, and find a roadmap to success. I have always been the kind of person who feels that in life relationships are everything. I've learned the best relationships are ones where there's an equitable give and take between all involved parties. Mr. Buckley is using a great number of tools and techniques to create and cement those kinds of relationships. The kind that lasts. The techniques in this book are purposeful ways to help anyone achieve their personal and organizational goals.

Jimmy E. Greene
CEO & President
Associated Builders & Contractors
The Greater Michigan Construction Academy

Table of Contents

Part Two - Mission

Part Three - Manifesto

I freed a thousand slaves. I could have freed a thousand more if only they knew they were slaves. — *Harriet Tubman*

Tip Off

When I was a kid, like many others, I experienced the "inner city blues." In my neighborhood, and others like it, the letters "O.G." stood for "Original Gangster." This moniker was given to those who were "deep" in the streets or had relative longevity in their waywardness. In my life, I have met some men (and a few ladies) who have carried this O.G. title. While it served its purpose for the title bearer in certain circumstances, it's what I call the old mindset. It's easy to think of someone as a common criminal, but these are some of the most intelligent people you could meet. They acquired their knowledge through the practical "hands-on" applications of living life. This is far more relevant than the canned textbook theory that's not always applicable growing up in some environments.

What do I consider an "O.G." today? Let's keep it real. There are some severe problems in our community. When I say in our community, I mean the black community. Solving these problems will take a new way of thinking. I'm about to turn everything you thought you knew upside down. Call it a mindset shift. "O.G.," meaning "Obtaining Greatness," is the new mindset. When you learn, you grow. But growth must be intentional. Most of the people I know that made it out of the "hood" did so because they learned their lesson and applied the lesson quickly.

Or at least quick enough that their foolishness didn't catch up with them. Or, they learned while away at boarding school, if you know what I mean. These lessons learned came with tremendous gratitude and appreciation and a lot of pain. It is like having a second chance at life. When you get a second chance you want to share what you know with others. You realize there are so many who didn't make it. You develop a "new" mindset.

My "O.G. - Obtaining Greatness" and "O.G. Tip of the Day" social media post prompted this book title and the tagline, "Change Your Mindset, Change Your Life." For years, my "O.G. Tip of the Day" social media posts would encourage and motivate me as I started each day. I am thankful for those who came along for the ride and were motivated too. This message is directed toward my followers and those who are or who were at one time living "that life." I didn't live that life; not to any extreme. You can't be a part-time gangster. You may have heard the saying, "Just because you're in a garage doesn't make you a car." Well, I was in the hood and understood the hood, but I never wanted to stay in the hood and by the grace of God I made it out of the hood. Now, I am there by choice helping others to be successful.

I'm giving you play by play guidance for winning this game. And although the game is to be sold and not told, we're going to flip that. I encourage readers to take this journey as I make relevant what separates the "haves" from the "have-nots." It's not all about money. This book gives you direction on how to make it out of the "hood," focusing on how you think. Are you living "that life?" What is your "hood?" Is it that dead-end job? Or is it a bad relationship? Your "hood" may not be physical in nature, but it's whatever you want to escape or transform into something great. "O.G. - Obtaining Greatness" thinking will change your circumstances by transforming your mind, not just your residence.

I wrote this book to make US great again

The United States of America is one of the most significant countries on earth. There's no other place I would want to be than in the U.S. I wrote this book from a black mans' perspective because black people hold a very substantial role in making this country great. I believe we must lead the charge to save our families and our communities. We know the problems, the laws in this book are a solution. I made it out of these same inner cities that have destroyed so many others despite the prominence of this nation and the inherent greatness within everyone.

The areas of my life I needed to address personally, and the areas the black community must address collectively, cannot be at the mercy of whether America addresses her issues. Unfortunately, there is a possibility she won't. If it has not happened in all this time, really? Do you think it will happen one day soon? Our communities are in trouble now. You (black people) are our only hope. There were people I knew from my neighborhood that were ten times as smart, far more articulate and had way more heart than I did that didn't make it out. It is my responsibility to give this knowledge back and help people, young and old, know that controlling how you think will allow you to change your future. It will also improve our culture.

I also want to share with the reader the importance of diversity and cultural awareness. We are all better together. Is there an area of your life that hinders you or a trap you want to make it out of? Have you ever thought there must be more to life? Have you always had this feeling of being so close, but could never grasp it? Let's focus on the solutions that can change your life. Greatness is in you.

This book is for anyone who wants to grow

This book was written for individuals that want to grow and understand their growth is their responsibility. They also know there is a direct correlation between their personal growth, the growth of their children and their children's children. Your personal growth correlates to the level of growth in your community. Generational blessings are in the balance. The reader of this book will understand even if you don't reap the harvest, it is imperative you plant the seeds. If you want to make a difference and more dollars, this book will help you do both. This book will keep you focused on attaining more meaningful and significant goals. If you are willing to change your mindset to grow to the next level, this book is for you.

This book is written from an African American perspective, but anyone can grow to "O.G." status. I speak directly to the black community, specifically black men, but these truths, when applied, will benefit any color, gender or creed. But, it would be a shame if these laws bypassed the intended audience and edified the rest of the world. To my brothers and sisters, let's try something different from what you are accustomed to. Most of us inherited these same core values but somehow forgot them over the last generation or two.

If you've ever listened to me speak on personal growth, or followed me on social media, you have a flavor of how this book provides different thinking that goes against the status quo. This book is anything but the same old mindsets. I want you to think like a chess grandmaster. Let us think ten steps ahead with contingencies. If I were coaching you I would not tell you what to do, but this book allows me to be a bit more direct. Don't get offended and reserve your judgment until the end. Growth hurts.

This book is not status quo thinking

A Chinese proverb said, "The best time to plant an oak tree was 100 years ago and the second-best time is today." This book is about accountability and putting in the time necessary to make right some of the wrongs in your life. It doesn't matter whose fault it is. What matters is that it's your responsibility to make change happen. If you keep on doing what you've done, you'll keep on getting what you have had in the past. This book does not sugar coat any problems you face. There are some hard truths and you might not like them. This is not your classic self-help book. Although I believe some principles endure and are timeless, it's our unique experiences that allow us to tell our individual stories in a way that resonates with others. I hope my stories and insights will give you a unique perspective into who you are, and what you already have inside of you. Greatness is in you and I need you to believe that. Believe it's also in our babies and our community. Status quo has got to go!

What are the benefits to the reader

There are several benefits for the reader including guidance in the areas of leadership, teamwork and executing. You might learn more about yourself than you want to. This will benefit not only you, but everyone connected to you. This is my definitive playbook full of tips and strategies that will allow our children and our grandchildren to be experts in taking tools and building anything they should ever want or need. "I need a job," has been a popular refrain in our inner cities. We will change this thinking to "I see an opportunity." "How much money can I make?" to "how many people can I help and give opportunities?" "How can I serve?"

This book is about your future. If you want to get rich quick, this book is not for you. If you're looking for someone to blame, again, this is the wrong book. Enough of us have dealt with the trauma of being black in America, or whatever cross you've had to bare. I think we are making progress. Arguing we have not come as far as we thought we had is arguing a moot point. We can make more progress; possibly more on our own than with the reluctant help of others. If you believe that, this book is for you.

How this book is structured

This book is written in three parts. Part I focuses on you the individual. It is your personal assessment of your O.G. strengths, or lack thereof, how you got to where you are now and what you will need to get where you want to go. It focuses on responsibility and accountability. It's the self-reflective part of the book that makes you look long and hard in the mirror before ever looking at anyone else. It's "all eyes on you."

Part II will focus on your crew. Your crew can be your family. It could be a team at work or any place where you have influence. Once you've dealt with any personal issues, we all have them, we can move to teach and share in our immediate circles. I've found when I'm showing or teaching others, the information or habits are solidified deeper within myself. This part of the book allows you to leverage your best self with the help of others. You want to arrive at a place where leadership is built into your DNA and begins to transform the DNA of everyone you're connected to.

Part III will show how the pieces fit together. What does an O.G. community look like with leadership built into its DNA? What does a family look like, or an organization? What you learn in parts one and two, are the foundation and framework for what you want to build and anything you want to outlast you. Part three is what I call the "Legacy Laws." O.G. is all about legacy, and if you're going to build something that will outlive you, this is the right book. I will use the terms "O.G." and "Obtaining Greatness" interchangeably, and from now on, O.G. has a new meaning in your life. Ok O.G., let's get started.

Part I - Mantra

If It's to Be, It's Up to Me

To be successful, you must take full responsibility for <u>your</u> actions.

Chapter 1 - Waiting to Excel
The Holding Law
Getting to know you

There will be delays on your journey. What you do during this time
has a significant impact on when you reach your destination.
Use your time wisely.

Hold on

Have you ever been "on hold?" Being placed on hold can seem like a waste of time for a busy professional. Anytime you are waiting for someone else, and it looks as though your needs should have been met a long time ago, it becomes very frustrating, to say the least. We all have, at times, had opportunities in our lives where there have been delays.

The Holding Law will show you a way to optimize this time and use it to our benefit. The Holding Law causes a delay in our life. In sports, if you are called for holding, there has been an illegal delivery on the part of the opponent. Has anyone ever told you to "hold tight?" Sometimes this is a deliberate effort to delineate you and your forward progress and momentum to benefit someone else. This is not someone else that you have chosen, but someone random that may or may not have your best interests.

Sometimes we are barely holding on. Have you ever been at your wits end and did not know how you would make it? If you are in this spot right now, let me encourage you to hold on. When you get through a couple of chapters of this book, you will see there is a divine order to what you have been going through. There are steps you can take to turn your mess into a success.

Standing Still

When my children were younger, flying with the family was always a very stressful situation. Although my family is not as large, I'm reminded of Macaulay Caulklin in the movie *Home Alone* where there is a headcount of each family member at various checkpoints leading to the destination. My routine is somewhat similar. In the airport, I'm always head counting. On one trip with a connecting flight through Atlanta's Hart International Airport, I came up short with my headcount!

There was a very short layover time between landing and takeoff. Just enough to make it from the arrival flight to the departing one. On the escalator, the headcount equaled "five." When we got off the escalator once again headcount, "five." Waiting on the plane train, the shuttle that takes passengers between terminals and concourses, headcount: "five." On the plane train headed to the next gate, headcount "four!" Second and third headcount: "four." Somehow my daughter did not make it on the plane train. I looked through the window and motioned for her to stay there! Don't move! That was the most anxiety filled five minutes of my life, and there was nothing I could do but return to the place we had just left. We exited the plane train and entered one traveling back to the gate we'd come from to find my baby girl right where I had left her.

If you are ever separated from your Heavenly Father, as soon as you realize you are out of His presence, or your vision is unclear, stand still. He'll find you. Also, how many times have you been in a rush only to see you needed to return to the place you left? The Holding Law teaches you patience. You have enough fuel to reach your destination. In this troubled world, we will continue in this holding pattern until we understand this principle. Unfortunately, some of us won't get it and will come dangerously close to running out of fuel. We will be diverted to land somewhere else, but not where God intended. You'll get to your destination eventually, but you prolong the time and add extra anxiety when there's this constant need to execute when you haven't been properly instructed.

Everyone has different circumstances and different reasons which cause them to continue flying in their various holding patterns. Some people you personally know could keep to their desired destinations seemingly with no delay. We have different stories and backgrounds. Your environment does play a part and I am sure most of us have come too far to turn back now. The good news is you are more than your circumstances and you are more than your environment. You are even more than your heredity. Holding on to God may not be "in style" as it was a generation ago. You must understand there is a reason for everything you are going through now and the circumstances are only there to mold and shape you; to prepare you for what is to come.

Listening to your inner voice

O.G., what is your purpose? I found myself asking this question almost 30 years ago. I was at a party, and as the bass pounded in sync with the body of the half-naked girl dancing in front of me, I'm thinking, "What am I doing here?" I'll admit it was not the best time for a young man to have an epiphany. Ever since I can remember, life-changing questions would pop into my head at the darnedest time. Someone said the two most important days in a person's life is the day you were born and the day you discover why you were born. Did you have someone in your life take you serious as a young person when you had a similar question or thought? The best that young lady would have done, had I told her, would be to find someone else who wanted to dance. I don't know if my mother would have known how to answer that question if I had posed it to her (she wasn't 30 years old yet).

Encourage self-reflection. It will provide context to your life. Each moment of your life will add to the minutes of joy, pain, suffering, and triumphs. These minutes become the hours of struggle and success. Then they become the days of different circumstances that are unique to you and me as individuals. We come from different environments, but it's the same process. I'm sure my epiphany was shared by very few that night, but at some point, everyone has it. We are raised in the same households, abide by the same rules, and have the same values instilled by our parents. Yet only by DNA can you tell some people are related. Your purpose is uniquely yours and it doesn't matter the environment or circumstances you are placed in. To discover what's your reason for being, you must sit still long enough.

Patience on Purpose

I never was an excellent Spades player. Or, maybe my partners weren't good players. Where I come from, this is a deal breaker. You either play or go home. As with anything else, there is a level of skill you want to bring to the table to enjoy the game, but learn on your own time. In life, we spend too much time trying to peak at the cards of our fellow players. Focusing on others is time taken away from planning our strategy to win. We're cheating ourselves if we try to trick others. We renege ourselves from the life God intended to bless us with. Sure, know what's being played, but do you know how silly it is to cheat yourself? We all know that guy who spends massive amounts of time and energy on one illegal scheme or another. And what do we say about that guy? "If he only spent half that time on something honest, he'd be very successful." Too bad for that guy, and unfortunately for some of us, cheating comes with penalties.

I was raised in an environment where a little lying was ok. I had a few friends with bad credit by age ten, and we became a pro at the "No, she ain't home" script. I say this because everyone has a different perception of what cheating is. There's a host of reasons why it may take longer for some of us than others to find our purpose, but once we discover it, that is just the beginning of the "wait." While you are "out" of purpose you are in dangerous territory.

There is a direct correlation between time spent out of purpose and the unpleasant circumstances we can find ourselves in; sometimes we even double down on those unpleasant circumstances. I know you would never do this, but do you have friends or family who've repeatedly made the same mistake or choices that further perpetuate an unpleasant circumstance? It seems no matter what they do the results continue to be the same.

Sometimes the actions, from the outside looking in, look like different choices. One of my favorites, "I'm moving away from this god-awful place. Everyone is hating on me." The funny thing about circumstance is no matter where we decide to relocate, voilà! There we are. I'm not stating that the environment doesn't play a part in how you develop. We are molded by our environment plus our heredity to a certain extent, but where you start is not where you must end. This is more of a mental exercise than physical. So how do we change and break the pattern that has been engrained in us for a generation or more?

Think and Grow Rich

I never knew my father as a young child growing up. My mom and I lived with her grandmother, my great-grandmother, and the only male influence I had in life were my uncles. They worked in sales. One uncle was often immersed in self-help literature and tapes to further his career. For my tenth birthday, he purchased me a copy of Napoleon Hill's epic book, "The Law of Success." The Law of Success is the monstrous thousand plus page life work from which the more popular "Think and Grow Rich" book was derived. Hill was charged by steel magnate Andrew Carnegie with interviewing successful business leaders to learn what made them successful. He spent the next 25 years doing so. My uncle purchased several copies of this book for his children, nieces, and nephews. I read it from cover to cover. This book, and others, led me to the Norman Vincent Peale's, Wayne Dwyer's and Brian Tracy's of the self-improvement world. We were not a New Age household by any means. If it was up to my great-grandma O.G. meant, "Only God!"

For my fifteenth birthday, I received a subscription to the Wall Street Journal. Yes, that's what I asked for. The stock market intrigued me and I had an affinity with numbers. Let me be clear, I didn't understand any of it, initially, but I had enough exposure to know what I wanted to be when I grew up. I wanted to be great. I wanted to be a stockbroker. Another book I read in my teens was "The Art of The Deal" by Donald J. Trump. I'm somewhat embarrassed to say this man was a hero of mine. I had a great-uncle, who was more like my granddad, who was a real estate investor. I watched him, and I noticed his life was vastly different from many of my other family members. Although he was an older man, I had a bond with him and was intrigued by him. He wasn't extravagant by any means. He was a General Motors (GM) retiree just like many other men I knew from the area (I lived in a GM town). But he and his wife always seemed to have more than enough. Almost everyone else I knew lived in "lack."

To further my own real estate dreams, I saved my money and purchased the "Carlton Sheets No Money Down Real Estate" course. I know you remember those late-night infomercials. But

21

wait, there's more! A family friend owned a neighborhood grocery store and my first job was as a stock boy (far from broker). I had my very first FICA paying, income tax filing, check cashing job at the young age of 15. I mowed lawns, raked leaves and shoveled snow. You'd think I would be a multi-millionaire by 30, definitely by age 40. I accumulated a few economic weapons in my war chest, but could never get past barely having enough to eat. Napoleon Hill, Donald Trump nor Carleton Sheets could save me from the process that had to happen to develop my mind and change the way I looked at life.

Something had to bridge the gap between circumstance; where I was, and opportunity; where I wanted to go. There needed to be a band that could accommodate the ebb and flow of the volatile inner city and keep me connected to my goals and the vision I had in my head. Something to keep that vision board from ending up being tucked away in the back of a closet. Unfortunately, the environment was far too appealing for me to escape unscathed and dropped a bomb on my childhood hopes and dreams. The Holding Law prevailed.

Can you hear me now?

As I maneuvered into my stance, squared to my target, I raised my firearm. Gripping it with my dominant hand and placing my finger on the trigger, I aligned my front sight looking through the rear and aimed at the target. Then I squeezed the trigger. If you've ever gone to a gun range or had the opportunity to fire a handgun, I'm sure you are familiar with ringing ears or even sometimes temporary deafness. Impairment is a side effect of not protecting our senses, in this case, our hearing. The great thing about a shooting range, at least the one I visit, is hearing protection is mandatory. Sometimes the circumstances in our lives are so loud you can't hear anything else. That temporary deafness may last longer than you expect. You are left to your own devices and instead of realizing the importance of hearing protection you think, "I can take it." Protecting your hearing is critical.

I believe in God and I think He speaks to me. You may call this an over-exaggeration of intuition, conscious or just coincidence but stay with me for a minute. I didn't always hear but there is a process I had to go through to gain my hearing. When you relieve your mind of focusing on the day to day trials of life, and intentionally listen for this voice, you mentally prepare for landing and preparation for the next leg of your journey. It's like when receiving boarding instructions in a busy airport. Sometimes the voice over the intercom is clear, other times distorted. Put down your headphones, food or other distractions. You will then know what to do if you listen closely. You will be on target, focused and ready to squeeze the trigger, or execute.

How do we make this law work for us? You may say, "I've been holding for 20 years it's too late for me now." I tell you it's never too late. The circumstances in your life are the vehicle that drives you to your appointed destination. Let me show you how "Holding" is worth the wait.

Buy and Hold

I've worked in the financial services world for almost two decades, and I have had clients get nervous if the stock market shows any signs of distress. They are glued to their television or financial website watching every index movement every day. I don't know about you, but I didn't grow wealth to worry every day. It's great to be at peace when everything around you is going haywire. Greatness is like a quality stock strategically placed in an investors' portfolio. It is defensive and can weather the turbulent storms of life; it also can pay healthy dividends. Have you ever watched a stock in your portfolio get beaten up so bad you could not take the pain anymore, then sell it? It's contradictory to think when you're experiencing the most pain, that at this point there's the greatest opportunity. And yes, you can purchase it again but the time is increased to reap the same reward if you would have just stayed in the holding pattern.

In the investment world, we use what's called an investment policy statement or IPS. This document will allow you to set the vision or plan for the various assets in your portfolio. It spells out different scenarios that can happen and details ahead of time what we will do about them. The Holding Law has its own IPS that allows you the ability to weather storms and keep focused on your vision. This is what I call your Internal Philosophy Statement. This is the guiding principle in your life. It must be internalized to be effective. For me, this is the Holy Scriptures. I believe it is God's Word and it has yet to fail me. Your IPS won't be exactly like mine. That's fine, just stay consistent.

I would love to say when I started on this path things changed overnight. They didn't. It was a process. A process that is internalized during a very patient period in your life. The upfront cost put into this process reduces unnecessary time spent circling your destination or destiny. You can't "time" the market.

You don't know where you will have ups or downs, neither can you "time" your life. Stuff happens. Your IPS keeps you in the higher probability scenarios that favor your long-term success. We will talk more about this in the next chapter. Once you get your IPS right, set it and forget it. Don't waver on your strategy. It's ok to be tactical, but stay rooted, in something. Let it work in your favor.

The Master of the Universe

As a child growing up in the inner city, I was always fascinated with astronomy. How did those planets stay in their exact orbit after millions of years? That's the type of patience God uses to train us for higher levels. Regardless of the circumstances, if you have the right mindset, you can develop a vision for what you want to accomplish.

Your Internal Philosophy Statement will allow you to feel and hear the storms of life without reacting to them. The IPS is an agreement drafted by the Creator and the client (You). Volatility is involved. The universe will do what it will. You must trust the process and hold to the vision that has been set forth according to your IPS. It's important to note your vision should be crafted in moments of clarity and calm, not fear and anxiety. Adhering to the Holding Law will allow what you really want to supersede what you think you want in the moment. Vision requires dedication.

I talk about God a lot. That's because He's such a large part of my life. The Holding Law is what kept me when I went through some of the most dangerous times in my life. It didn't matter how smart I thought I was. Every move I made outside of the God-given vision required me to wait. This wait was longer than originally planned. After enough time passes by you learn your lesson. So, when you hear "opportunity" calling that is not a part of your vision, you can respond, "No thanks. I'll wait." Although I may have been temporarily disappointed and feeling as though I may have been missing out on whatever it was my friends were getting into at the time, it never failed the next day the only thing I missed was trouble.

Disappointment

Nothing forges character like disappointment. People watch you on the stage of life and get a glimpse of who you are. One definition of character is who you are when no one's looking. We can manipulate the actor who is on stage. We can change his lines, we can change costumes, and we can also have a do-over for even higher performance, but our character is rarely ever shaped in public. It's those crying nights, and in those times of wondering why, that force us to look within instead of for an external reason.

One of my earliest disappointments as a child growing up was when my dog Blacky died. If you are a pet owner, I know you understand the grief this causes. If you're not a pet owner, it's just like losing a family member; someone who is faithful and always has your back. Blacky was a straight "hood" canine. "Awe! May I pet him?" "No! That might not be a good idea." It was not a natural death. Someone shot Blacky. One of the unfortunate things about his demise is his life probably could have been saved. It may have been a pellet gun that wounded him, and with adequate veterinarian care, I'm sure my dog's fate could have been avoided. So Blacky's death was an economic decision. One that would shape my life and put me on a path that caused me to seek abundance in whatever way I could, good or bad.

I never wanted my essential happiness and contentment to be dictated by money, or the lack thereof. This incident in my life placed me in a holding pattern and limited me emotionally. I didn't want to be that close to anyone or anything again. At that point in my life, I had not experienced the death of anyone significant in my life, and at that age, I did not know how to process it.

Can you recall a situation in your life that shaped your behavior for years to come? Sometimes it's not as evident until we take a thoughtful look at our action. Other times it's not apparent to us until it is pointed out by someone else. The key is self-awareness. Once you allow yourself to recognize what has happened in your life and the repercussions because of it, you are on the road to a smooth landing and a timely arrival to your destination. My grandma used to say, "He may not come when you want Him, but He is always on time." I found this to be true in my life and when you acknowledge this, you can flow and graciously maneuver around or through whatever circumstances you find yourself in. In fact, you will see your life moving at speeds faster than you may be accustomed to.

Hyper Drive

I love fast roller coasters. From the moment I hit the park, I am ready to go. The anticipation of the ride and the excitement of hearing other people scream is pure joy. You may or may not like roller coasters as I do, but have you noticed how the preparation for the ride lasts far longer than the trip itself? When we are adequately prepared, we make the right adjustments and make sure we are in the right line for the right vehicle. When we purchase our tickets for the speed lane, the preparation allows us to move faster and enjoy the ride sooner than we expected. The key is the preparation. I am learning to appreciate the process from the minute I step in line until I stepped out of the car at the end of the exhilarating ride. I love it all.

When you learn to enjoy the ride of life, you become more accustomed to multiple trips and enjoy them on a regular basis. I did not get to the point where I enjoyed roller coasters the way I do now overnight. How did I learn the process? It's like preparing for life. It's difficult, but worth it if you're doing what you love. Every amusement park trip, my goal was always to ride the newest coaster. Goal setting and preparation go hand in hand. To prepare for the task we are attempting to accomplish, or for any challenge life may bring us, there needs to be a systematic way of organizing and preparing our resources. It's not something we can take a half-hearted scatterbrain effort at doing. It must be done in an intelligent and orderly manner. When done correctly, we can speed the process and allow even more thrilling experiences in our lives.

S.M.A.R.T. O.G.

I read a quote by Venus Williams that said, "Set realistic goals, keep reevaluating, and be consistent." For those of you who have worked in corporate America or have spent any time reading any leadership literature, you are familiar with S.M.A.R.T. goals. If you don't know what S.M.A.R.T. goals are, S.M.A.R.T. is an acronym which stands for Specific, Measurable, Attainable, Realistic, and Timely.

A specific goal has a definite achievement in the end. It's not vague or defined in a way that is easily misinterpreted or forgotten. I want to lose weight is not a S.M.A.R.T. goal. It's not specific, but if you were to add you want to lose 35 pounds by summer not only have we added a measurable element, we've also added a time frame. If we said "July 1" it is more specific. If you only weigh 110 pounds that goal may not be realistic for you. The goal is attainable when action steps are involved, like working out three times a week.

Smart goals are divided into intervals. These intervals represent time frames. For example, one to three years would represent short-term goals. Three to five years would serve mid-term goals and five to ten years would be our long-range goals. This time factor is relative. I would recommend you take your short-term goals and monitor them over months or weeks depending on the activity. You can weigh yourself once a week, but you want to control what you eat every day. Don't weigh yourself every hour. The best way to monitor and achieve your long-term financial goal is through budgeting. Write down all your financial transactions for at least a month. Do you have more income than outgo?

To make your goals real they must be written down. After you have written them down, they must be placed somewhere you will see them every day. Consider making your goals part of your vision board or your planning calendar. Watch the man or woman who has specific, measurable, attainable, realistic goals that are timely and compare him to the man or woman that does not. You will see a dramatic difference in their holding patterns. The goal-oriented person will have more direct flights. Less time circling in the air and less time spent in layovers. Your goals will not be the same as your friend's goals. They will not be the same as your parent's goals. Your flight plan is uniquely yours and your life is a one-of-kind original. A masterpiece takes time and that's what the Holding Law demonstrates. Are you ready to master time?

As a young man I struggled with patience. I made rash decisions that took me off course and kept me "holding." Because of my lack of patience, I even ran out of gas and had to be diverted to other "airports" and risked crashing. Achieving your goals will take patience and to maximize our time we must fall in love with the process. It's exhilarating initially, but takes a lot of hard work and diligence to maintain. I struggled to understand how my best laid plan could still take far longer than I expected. I know the plan was still needed and fit in a greater program that was yet to be revealed at the time.

Time is our most precious commodity. You can lose all your money and all your worldly possessions, but if you have enough time you can certainly get all that back. But, if we run out of time, all the material goods in the world won't make one difference in your life. One day I saw a U-Haul following a hearse. It tickled me because I knew it was only a coincidence and they were not going to the same destination. When you master time you are increasing your life. When you are young time is on your side and we only spend time in a holding pattern to the extent we refuse to patiently find our purpose. Sometimes we discover our life's meaning and the clock starts ticking. It looks like time is working against us, but I found out it's the exact opposite. Once we find our purpose our life can shift into hyper drive and we will travel to places faster than we ever believed possible. Finding our purpose is how we get the Holding Law working in our favor. We go from fighting the system to embracing a different order and it makes all the difference.

Can you wait to be Great?

Janet Jackson dominated the late eighties with chart-topping hit after hit. I remember those times well and she was one of my favorite artist at that time. But the initial Janet I remember, as a young boy, was on one of my favorite television shows with James and Florida Evans and their sons Michael, JJ and daughter Thelma. Janet Jackson played a little girl named Penny. The show aired in the late 1970s. For ten years or so Janet had fallen off my radar. I had forgotten about Janet. That is until I heard her album "Control" and a song entitled "Funny How Time Flies When We're Having Fun." I love the French language, and some lyrics are spoken in French. Another great hit from that album was "What Have You Done for Me Lately?" Then there was "The Pleasure Principle." These songs all have one thing in common and that's time.

Delayed gratification

Wealthy people count every penny. It's part of their IPS, part of their character. Character will allow you to redeem time. Character is developed over time and its relative to your level of obedience. Obedience to God, obedience to your vision, or budget. Obedience to those who hold you accountable and compliant to the greatness that's within you. Greatness is within you. You are coming out of your holding period and into a place where the skills you've acquired over the years will become more meaningful, allowing you to begin pouring into others. You don't want to ignore the Holding Law. This law, once abided, will let you make up lost time and teach you to move with greater acceleration.

Unlike past trials and setbacks, once you are in sync with your declared vision, you will notice even in failure you will fail forward. Your failures will not hold you back, but miraculously, you will be propelled. When you're in sync with the God-given purpose for your life, you will learn to and want to fail as much as you can. Not intentionally, but by way of losing the fear that stops you from attempting to accomplish your bigger goals. You will conquer the doubt that keeps you from trying.

The people who don't fail are the people without worthwhile goals. Your holding period will only last if you kick against it. Let it go! Put what you think you want aside long enough to figure out your reason for being. This is not the end of the struggle. Life happens sometimes and the difference will be how you deal with it. I will end this chapter with a story about my friend Bill (not his real name).

Bill was brilliant growing up both academically and practically. Bill had beautiful parents who poured into his life daily. Bill was not from my neighborhood and went to private school. He had relatives that lived near me. Bill made a mistake hanging out with the wrong crowd. His taste for inner city excitement over mundane suburbia was perplexing. He lived a life that would cause his early demise if he didn't change his ways. He was really "out there." Although he was not economically challenged in any way, a drug conviction placed Bill in a holding pattern. This was devastating to everyone who knew Bill because these actions were not in line with his upbringing. It was one of those "mistakes" though not fatal, changes the trajectory of one's life seemingly in a negative way, but not necessarily. Bill was released a few months ago.

Sometimes our "cell" is the only thing that keeps us alive. Some of our holding periods are far longer. I know mine was even though it was not a physical cell. Never underestimate The Holding Law. I can't wait to see Bill's vision unfold. I can't wait to see your vision unfold. Delay your gratification. Greatness is in you!

To excel, you must be patient. Everything that has occurred in your life has happened for a reason. If we spend time questioning our circumstances and questioning why situations unfolded the way they did, we will waste even more time. It's all a process and right now we are learning the rules of the game.

We are learning the rules of engagement. Just understanding the rules will allow you to move at speed faster than you ever imagined you could go. I wonder what would happen if you mastered the rules of the game? How would that influence how you see yourself now? What if you could see yourself in the future? What if you believed that you have what it takes to accomplish everything you set out to achieve and you will meet every goal you have set for yourself? We will explore in Chapter 13 how your life will come full circle and you will understand everything that happened, had to happen.

Even if life seems a little bit out of control right now, if we could learn to relax and float we can reserve our strength, and listen for that still small voice that navigates us to our destiny. O.G., listen carefully, write it down and follow the instructions. You don't want to repeat the steps because you decided to go without instructions, do you? Patience and following guidelines keep you from going to the back of the line.

O.G. Code - "Why" wait

This is not a question, but an observation that waiting is the process by which we discover our "Why." Right now, it seems like it's all about you. Ultimately, it's not. But we need to help ourselves before we can help anyone else. The flight attendant tells you this before you take off. Keep in mind the following, as you determine what is your "Why."

- Greatness is within you.
- Where you start does not matter. Right now, your mind can't handle where you will end up.
- Learn to be proactive and not reactive.
- You didn't get where you are overnight. Take the time to allow God to reveal your purpose.
- Your vision is larger than you. You just can't see it right now. Don't rush it. Patience will make a winner out of you.
- Everything that has happened in your life can be made profitable. The fact you're still here is a testament to this.
- Everything great is a work in progress. Finished goods are just that, finished.
- If you took the time to mess it up, take the time to think it through.
- This is chess not checkers. Know your tenth move and all contingencies. It will only come with practice.
- There is a process. Trust the process. Be consistent.
- Pray for guidance to determine your "Why."

33

Conclusion

Let's go back to my investment analogy. Dollar cost averaging is an investment method where you invest the same dollar amount each specified period. This can be a very lucrative investment strategy versus the lump sums we may invest sporadically. The difference between the two approaches is consistency.

When you are operating within a given amount of time, you magnify the effectiveness of your holding period experience with consistency. Time is the great equalizer and steadfastness is like a turbo booster for you and for your effort. You may not be the best or greatest just yet but be consistent. Consistency will compound your efforts and give you the opportunity to make up for lost time. Excellence is not what you do sometimes but what you do consistently. It's not the one time one hit wonder we are trying to accomplish.

We are Obtaining Greatness and the way you become a true O.G., it must be in your blood, your DNA if you will. When you change your mindset, you accept the fact a blood transfusion is in order. I might not be your type. The real ones, those who master their universe and don't get caught in the BS, they don't have ice water running through their veins. They have a spirit of excellence running through them and their blood type is O.G. positive.

Ninety-nine percent of the failures
come from people who have the
habit of making excuses.

— *George Washington Carver*

Chapter II - Spirit of Excellence
The KeyStone Law
Set a standard for your life

What you use as your moral foundation must withstand the weight of your life's circumstances. Build on solid ground.

Who are you? Do you ever sit down and have a conversation with yourself about some of the choices you've made? Are those choices really yours? Or, are you unintentionally floating down the river of life, content with wherever it takes you?

When I was a young man I followed the "crowd." I hung out with the older guys in my neighborhood and they had an influence on me (for better or worse), and I had less impact on them. I was a very bright kid and was exposed, through my love of reading, to many things none of my homeboys were presented with. I was far better than I pretended to be. I see smart kids today suffering from this same peer pressure and it is heartbreaking the amount of talent we have in our young people that goes untapped! Sometimes I was the smartest kid in class. I say this not to pride myself but to point out I didn't have anyone to hold me accountable to a higher standard. I set the rule and I didn't have to stretch to do so. These early successes in my life left me in a place of stagnation.

Who holds you accountable?

I never liked asking for help. Do you remember sitting in class and you did not know the answer, but you were not going to raise your hand and ask either? I would dread being called on, and mastered the art of giving my instructor just the right amount of attention and eye contact showing enough confidence that I may know the answer. I knew they got a kick out of calling on those who didn't want to be called on. I said to myself, "Ma'am, I know you see these other hands up. Why are you calling on me?" This is another one of those cases of expending more energy for the cover-up than what it would take to confront the problem head-on. The problem is, I don't know the answer. The solution, ask questions.

Most of us only want to be accountable to ourselves and in our minds, this is the right thing to do. How do you look at being independent? Do you view asking for help as being dependent and weak? It's really the opposite. In Stephen Covey's book, "The 7 Habits of Highly Effective People," he provides a framework for living an effective life. He divides that framework into three parts. They are private victory, public victory and renewal. Within the seven laws you can find yourself in one of three states; dependent, independent and interdependent. You heard rapper Meek Mills say, "There's levels to this," yep, he was right. Unfortunately, most of us get stuck on the state of independence.

Wait, this is a good thing, right? I-N-D-E-P-E-N-D-E-N-C-E, you sing about it. You celebrate it. It's the "be all, end all." Maybe when you were of that old mindset, but now you are an O.G. – Obtaining Greatness. If you can support yourself, that's good. "Great," is when we can support ourselves and others too. We support each other. The sum is more than the parts. We're collaborating. If you instantly thought to yourself, "At least I'm not depending on someone else," I would challenge you to check your thinking. I think it is helpful to build our frame according to where we want to go and not where we have been. This keeps you marching forward and prevents you from getting stuck. Accountability is the first step on your path to interdependence, and the rest of the steps lay within what I call the KeyStone Law.

The KeyStone Law

In society, various cultures are governed by acceptable guidelines and behaviors that allow for peace and civility among its members. Likewise, we as individuals must adhere to the same structure in our personal lives for inner peace. The problem occurs when pride, arrogance and other negative personality traits keep us from setting a standard for better behavior and increased accountability. Pride comes before destruction. Decreasing everything and everyone to increase yourselves is a telling sign the Keystone Law is not operating in your life. What is this law? I'm glad you asked.

In my life, I have learned how to navigate and move in different social circles. This has allowed me the opportunity to check my values and morals against something more significant than the small circle I come from. I've also learned, on a professional level, ethics and fiduciary responsibility that far exceeded anything I had known growing up in my family, or interacting in my neighborhood.

We make conscious decisions on the standards we adhere to in our lives if we want to obtain greatness. I've had to unlearn much miseducation in life. Street code, womanizing and selfishness replaced with genuine godly character and respect for others. You grow to a point where a little bit of poison is still too much.

The Keystone Law bares the weight of our fortification. It is the code of conduct you should respect and follow to keep on your path to greatness. In a nutshell, it's what you think, what you do and who you surround yourself with. It's your philosophy. It consists of three weapons to guard you and your mind (change your mindset, change your life) against any challenge that comes against your O.G. - Obtaining Greatness mindset. Those three weapons are:

1. Your Attitude - how you think

2. Your Rituals - what you do

3. Your Mastermind - who you surround yourself with

Proper attitude brings with it accountability. I remember when I began speaking professionally. I had a tough time finding my groove. I had attended various training and seminars not to mention online courses, books, and YouTube. Technically, I was well prepared. I had all the tools and had trained with some of the best in the industry. It wasn't until I made a mental correction, realizing I couldn't do it on my own, that I was able to go to the next level. This realization came through listening to a trusted mentor.

If your dream can be accomplished by yourself, you're not dreaming big enough. It's too easy to slip into procrastination or doubt your abilities when there is no one there to push you forward. The attitude of me, myself and I must change. How do you turn this view? Is it really that important? The answer is a resounding YES!

Attitude

Everyone knows someone with a bad attitude. In the Keystone Law, I'm not talking about negative or positive. That is too elementary. We're talking about greatness here. If you are struggling with whether you should or shouldn't be a positive person, at best you are aiming for "average." The attitude I'm referring to has more to do with submitting to your values. No one is perfect, and there are offensive traits in the best of us and virtuous traits in the worst of us. We need a plan and a willingness to see ourselves now.

My supervisor was an older man and he made a remark that could be construed as racist. I emphasize "could" because he was a great guy. Was there something deep down inside from days gone by? Possibly. I bring this up not to focus on his misstep but on the choices I had in handling it. I didn't make a big deal about it. I gave him the benefit of the doubt and chose to continue having a great work environment. If what you're telling me doesn't make a difference in my life one way or the other, I assume you're telling the truth and are a decent person. If you prove otherwise, that is a different story. But, your lie will not allow me to see all people as liars. Your attitude is the lens you see the world through. The truth is we can see whatever we choose to look at. Why not paint a picture of what you want versus one of what you don't want? I have some black friends that will see racism in everything. If all the front seats are full on the bus - racism. Outstanding warrant, racism. Baby mama takes them to court for child support? Racism! How? Well, the judge was white.

This is not the O.G. attitude and is part of what we want to eradicate. Likewise, many of my white friends can't see racism in anything and can have the wildest justifications for the disparities we see every day. How do you deal with touchy subjects? Do you get uncomfortable and shy away? Do you get defensive and stand your ground? Are you a facilitator and seek both sides of an argument? The inability to walk in another's shoes stops us from fostering the kind of relationships needed to break down barriers that separate people.

Empathy

The ability to walk in another man's shoes will take you a long way in life. Empathy allows greater understanding between those with differences of opinion. This is a fundamental element of effective communication, and I like the way Stephen Covey put it, "Seek first to understand, then to be understood." Unfortunately, this element of communication is almost nonexistent in our present-day discourse. Scenes of people talking over one another trying to get their point across is all but uncommon. Remember the subtitle of this book; "How to change your mindset so you can change your life."

The O.G. - Obtaining Greatness way is seeking first to understand. This can be difficult. Everyone wants to be heard, everyone wants to be understood. Although difficult, this is a very effective tool to have in one's toolbox, especially in marriage. You could make the argument that our ego gets in the way of our communication. In the book of Luke 6:28 it reads, "bless those that curse you and pray for them who despitefully use you." This scripture is not a license for someone to use you as a doormat. When you are actively on the offensive for what you want in life, you'll need less defense against what you don't want. If you are moving in the right direction, momentum will begin to work in your favor. Consistently move in the right direction. Develop the right type of consistent and constant behaviors.

Rituals

The alarm on my phone begins the default Samsung jingle at 4:30 a.m. I slide out of bed onto my knees for a half hour of prayer. Then I get up, walk to my reading room for another 15 to 30 minutes of meditation consisting mostly of breathing exercises. I'll have a piece of fruit before I leave the house and walk the 1.5 miles twice around my subdivision. Sometimes I'll run, depending on my mood and how my prayer and meditation went. When I return home, I will get back in bed to cuddle with my wife until she's ready to get up and we'll get dressed together. I pray with my children before they go to school and I drive them. This is how I started my day for many years. Every day I try to keep the same sequence in the morning and get to bed at the same time each night. Every day I attempt to write at least 1,500 words. Sometimes I will do a lot more, but this minimum amount allows me to continue to flow in my writing. This ritual will enable me to maintain my flow in life.

If you are in a place where your schedule is a jumbled mess of inconsistent functions and activities, it is safe to assume your life will follow suit. I have grown to a place where the "peace of mind" gained from these rituals is not up for negotiations. Thoughts, actions, habit, and character in that order, are the building blocks to greatness. The KeyStone Law allows us to look in the mirror and judge ourselves against criteria we select for ourselves. We are not trying to live up to the expectations of others. This walk is a personal journey.

Everyone's rituals are different. What works for the stay-at-home mom with three kids will be completely different from the woman who's a partner at her law firm. The key is to find what works then fine tune it into a process, or system, that can be easily duplicated and learned by you. Your rituals should be defined enough to meet your goals yet flexible so you meet unexpected challenges. It's better if you decide to work out three days a week, and then if time allows, squeeze in an extra day than to set the bar too high. You know you can't consistently meet a schedule to work out six days a week.

If you are a morning person and your spouse is a night owl, a little extra effort should go into planning to ensure you both have adequate quality time together. That quality time will also be a ritual. Set two or three routines for ending your night together. Discuss your day, pray, or cuddle. Do whatever enhances your quality time. Attending weekly church service has been a defining ritual in my life. Sometimes I don't want to go, but the ritual is ingrained in me and my family. This affects different points and aspects of my life. I always feel better afterward. It gives my family one more weekly opportunity to get together.

Positive rituals will provide even more incidental benefits you don't recognize. Sunday dinner at Big Ma's provides a lot more than a delicious meal. Relationships are strengthened. Without that dinner, how many times throughout the week would you make or have time to see everyone you normally see on Sunday? We are better together.

The O.G.'s Mastermind

Interdependence can be hard for us but it doesn't have to be. When you have a desire to obtain the greatness that is already on the inside of you, you grow to the point of desiring to pour into others. Once you have "made it," you have a desire to see others make it. Have you ever held back from seeking help from someone who has traveled the road you are headed down? "They could never have time for me," you tell yourself. When someone really lives this O.G. lifestyle, they want nothing less than to share their knowledge with someone else. You are not in this for yourself. This is bigger than you and real O.G.'s know this. Again, when we connect, we become greater than our sum individually. This is a powerful principal when applied correctly. This is the power of the Mastermind.

If you don't have anyone near you to rub elbows with your mastermind can start in your imagination. Yes, you can use your imagination to grow and develop. Who, living or dead, would you like to have a conversation with if you could? What profound questions would you ask? This may be someone you want in your mastermind. How do you pull this off?

When I was a kid, I had a mastermind group consisting of the Justice League of America. I would choose a superhero to emulate running the meeting to solve the problems of the world. If you had the imagination now that you had when you were a kid, you could probably create the next iPhone. My mastermind today is a little different. I have a physical mastermind of trusted advisors and a mental mastermind. These individuals allow me to see growth from varying perspectives and enable me to tap into wisdom I need to reach and keep O.G. status. I will share my mental O.G. - Obtaining Greatness mastermind with you.

At the head of my table, Dr. Martin Luther King, Jr. He sits opposite me and is symbolic of passing the torch of the civil rights era, which symbolized social and political power (His assassination preempted the push for economic power). I also have my fraternity brother, the late Reginald Lewis former CEO of TLC Beatrice International epitomizing knowledge of corporate America. Sitting beside me is Tupac Shakur and Harriet Tubman. The team rounds out with Malcolm X and Madame CJ Walker, the first self-made female millionaire.

Each of these individuals have unique qualities to assist me in accomplishing my goals. There are some powerful communicators at this table. I embody the spirit of Harriet Tubman and her role in history. I hold to one quote attributed to her, "I would have freed a lot more if they knew they were slaves." We will revisit this throughout the text.

Take a minute and write down twelve people, dead or alive, who you need help from to accomplish your goal. Think carefully about why they are beneficial to you and which attributes of their character you would like to embody. After you have written this list, ask yourself, "Who do I know right now that I have access to with the trait or quality I seek?" You have access to many mentors even if you don't have weekly access, or any access to their time. The age of the internet! Google who you would like to study. Read their books, watch their videos and try emulating them. Exercising your imagination is just like exercising your body.

The KeyStone Law is almost magical. You combine your

spiritual and mental faculty with your everyday routines. This allows you consistent adherence to the standards you set for yourself. You are now wearing the proper uniform and equipment to maximize your effectiveness. Don't allow your natural fears to keep you from imagining. As children, we are very good with our imaginations. As time goes by, however, this faculty diminishes greatly, and we find ourselves limited in thinking of anything outside of the status quo. Our imagination allows us to see the outcome before it materializes. The question becomes, "What outcome are you seeing?" This is important because it builds your faith and your belief in having the power to accomplish your goal. Your imagination sets your foundation for abundance. The right Attitude, Rituals and Mastermind; consider yourself A.R.M.ed!

A.R.M.ed for Abundance

The right attitude, the proper rituals, and your mastermind is a recipe for abundance. The abundant mindset recognizes there is always enough and lack must cease to exist in your world. There are different seasons we go through in life and, depending on your path, the abundant mindset appears sooner for some. Here are three questions to ask that will tell if you're thinking with the abundant mind.

1. Does you circle consist of growth-minded individuals?

Outside of your mastermind you will need real people to help you in your day to day journey. There is only so much you can accomplish alone. We will talk more about your crew in Part II. For now, focus on the critical two to five people you trust and have a commitment to (if you have trust issues stay with me), and who are committed to as well. The important point is they all have growth mindsets. When a S.W.A.T. team enters a building it's not done willy nilly. They are "of one mind and on one accord." Many of the ideas presented here in this book can be outside most of your friends and families comfort zone. When people see you have made a change, especially those who are close to you, you may sense some stress in the relationship. We do not want to add to it by bragging about our mastermind or sharing our great goals out loud. Remember, <u>iron</u> sharpens <u>iron</u>. Watch who you rub against.

2. What are your expectations?

Are you a nose tackle or a wide receiver? I speak often about how our community does a great job playing defense. We have a natural guard that stays up and sometimes rightfully so (except when it comes to our money, more in chapter eight). You won't let anything through. If you're never in a position to receive, how will we ever catch anything? Yes, the opponents defense has been strong but I challenge you to analyze his offense. When you have an O.G. - Obtaining Greatness mindset, you understand someone's defense is no excuse for your lousy offense. Focus on winning. Expect to receive, expect to score.

3. Do you find yourself speaking "lack" language?

Words like "always," "never," "can't," or "won't" can be signs of a "lack" mentality. ("I never seem to get promoted." " I always come up short." " There's never any help.") This language becomes a self-fulfilling prophecy and paints your destiny. If you are not careful this can slip up on you. You will find yourself speaking in a tenor, that if you were to stop and listen to yourself, you know that's not the real you. But, as time goes on, if we've become lazy and not deliberate in how we control our speech it becomes a habit. Words are very important. You have the vocabulary to articulate everything negative but come up short on the positive; the growth, expansion and opportunity. You will speak "lack" language by default if you don't have the tools, or words, to say otherwise.

A.R.Med for Growth

What is your growth plan? This is a question I had to answer when I discovered my life skills, though they were up for the task at hand, were not adequate for where I wanted to go in the future. I had to understand what got me "here" would not take me "there." For over 40 years leadership guru John Maxwell has A.R.M.ed leaders all over the world with strategies for growth and effective leadership. In his book, "The 15 Laws of Growth," John teaches that growth should be a deliberate part of a person's life. It is a process. We can't be led to believe it just happens by default. That is not the kind of growth that allows you to achieve greatness.

If you're content with good, I challenge you to stretch for more. Growth is not always comfortable. If you ever played sports and were a part of a great team, you know you pushed harder in practice than what you had to in some games. Growth had to happen before you got into the spotlight. If you have an attitude that searches for self-improvement, and you put in place the rituals that will allow you to become skillful, over time you can utilize your accountability partners and role models to achieve growth in any area of your life.

W.I.N.G. Tips (Where I need growth)

If you are honest with yourself, there are some areas in your life where you are secure and other regions where you are weak. I always encourage folks to build on their strengths. If there are weaknesses that are holding you back, you will need to grow those areas. Here are some questions you should ask yourself when developing your growth plan.

1. What's the big picture telling you?

You want to recognize where your strengths lie and build those strengths. I like to separate strengths into two categories: personal and professional. Although there is a lot of overlap between the two, excellence in one does not mean excellence in the other. You know that thriving business professional that climbs the ranks to CEO or builds his business from the ground up? From the outside, he's on top of the world. He has the money, prestige and social accolades that accompany success. If you look a little closer, things aren't always what they seem. In many cases, second, third and even fourth wives are common.

The professional strengths which allow you to rise to the top in the business world won't heal or nurture your family. Your professional strengths, in many cases, aren't strengths at all if it destroys your family. Balance your professional strengths with personal strengths. Personal strengths cause you to ask, "Is this ladder I'm climbing leaning against the right wall?" "Is the price I'm paying for my success worth the pain?" In many cases, the answer is no and you will need to reassess your priorities. Asking the tough questions is a strength and ignoring what's important is a weakness whether you are at home or at work.

2. What are your roles?

You wear many hats in your life and you don't want to wear more than what you can maintain with a spirit of excellence. It is better to do one thing great than a lot of things average. Find the critical roles in your life you want to excel in and consider releasing some of the positions where you can't excel. This is a tough call because you are pulled in many different directions and you feel things won't get done if you don't do them. These may be "good" roles and you're doing "good" work, but the greatness in your life cannot be at the mercy of the good. If you let this happen over time, it will lead to you having more frustration with your lot in life. This is because you won't walk in your true purpose due to lack of clarity and direction. It's hard to see when there's too much clutter.

3. What do you want to change?

Once you discover your purpose, you will find areas in your life you operate in that don't fit your goals and life objectives. The holding law will continue working in your life as long you wish to remain attached to an area that is outside of your purpose. This makes it very important to change areas that are taking valuable fuel resources from areas that deserve more attention.

Change is always difficult and to the degree you embrace change, you will distance yourself from "good" to embrace "great." Sometimes it takes external influence to provoke needed change in your life. What you eat, drink or smoke changes only after your doctor has made an unfavorable prognosis. You want to get ahead of the inevitable. Change is going to happen, like it or not. If you decide how it happens, you are showing signs of growth. If you bend over and stick your head in the sand then you put yourself in a position for something uncomfortable to happen.

4. What's your "Why?"

What is the most important reason that gets you up in the morning? Knowing your "why" will allow you to move past willpower and develop staying power. It's easy to put too much confidence in your will to get over. If you don't ask "why" the "will" won't. Keep your "why" in front of you and allow it to dictate what's important according to your purpose. You must be honest with yourself concerning your "why," or you will make excuses. I know a guy who likes to justify every action he makes which is contrary to his goals. Every year the goal post is moved further and further back, and he always has a reason for the setback. I always tell myself, it's terrible when you fool others, but when you begin to fool yourself, you're in big trouble.

A.R.M.ed for Battle

The KeyStone Law varies for different people. Personally, I weigh all my decisions and live my life according to the Word of God as found in the Holy Scriptures. This works for me (and a billion others). If the level of greatness you want to obtain was easy, you'd have it by now. I need all the help I can get.

If you have mastered your physical environment, meaning you have all the money you need, can be leisure in your time and experience good health, without a higher power, I applaud you. You may be a genius or have a very solid mental state (they say genius is close to insanity). I can't wait to read your book! I think you have lived long enough to know if you are not in a "storm," you have just come out of one, or you will experience one in the future. You can't escape it. Sometimes it feels like a spiritual war is going on in your life. One of my favorite Scriptures is Ephesians 6:11. It talks about putting on the "whole armor of God."

Do you know everything you encounter in life will not yield willingly to your command? When you see great people or organizations make it through the toughest challenges, you might wonder, "How did they do it? What's in their 'secret sauce'?" You will encounter situations in life that are far above anything you can handle with your earthly understanding. At the O.G. - Obtaining Greatness level you know when to fight, what weapons to fight with and you also know when the battle is not yours. What's your higher power?

Boundaries are good for you

My friend has a German Shepherd named King that roams freely around their home on about two acres. The dog will circle the perimeter of the house unchained but does not go past a certain distance. My friend has an electric dog fence installed. The dog wears a collar that will deliver an electric shock, just enough to get King's attention, when the transmitter detects King is getting out of range. This shock is training him where he can and cannot go. I can imagine it took King a couple zaps before he figured it out. How many times does life have to zap us before we figure out the further we stray from our purpose, outside the guidance of our vision, the more we become prey to the distractions of life? We always think we can handle more than we can. I heard one preacher say it like this: "Sin will make you go too far, stay too long and pay far more than what you intended to." We can become prodigal sons and daughters to our own visions only to one day realize we're off track. There are places in our lives that need correcting. The KeyStone law will keep you from wandering outside the parameters you set for yourself.

Blind spots

I was driving a rental car from the airport and I wasn't used to the bells and whistles this car had. As I'm driving down the road, I keep hearing this ding sound on occasion. I noticed it happened whenever I passed or was passed by other cars. I mentioned it to my wife when I got home and she said, "Oh that's just your blind spot detector. It tells you when there is something there you might not see."

The KeyStone law, when you adhere to it, will alert you to situations that may be creeping up on you. It will also give you a warning when you are getting a little too close to something. It's interesting how this works. Our attitude provides power to numerous sensors around us. You are open to outside information. You are teachable and not a "know-it-all." Those sensors are your mastermind. There is a learning mechanism that becomes more accurate with experience. This is the experience of our rituals. The longer we are true to our routines the more precise the system. The more inline our attitude is with the vision for our lives, the faster the response to our mastermind principles. You can always adjust your routine or have sub-routines for various responsibilities.

The KeyStone Law provides rules, procedures and guidance that give you a safety net. Excellence is color blind and can be a great equalizer. I will stress that this is one of the more important laws but it will only work if you work it.

O.G. Code - Take the Keys

The KeyStone law unlocks foundational truths that have propelled men and women to greatness for centuries. Age old wisdom and principles don't change. This is a strong foundation to build on.

- Remember, attitude is everything. Having the faith and discipline to change how we see things is powerful.
- Changing how you think will change how you feel. When you think differently, you will have the energy to manifest your greatness.
- Your attitude can affect others and can also be influenced by others. Be careful of the latter.
- Use your rituals to strengthen your mental and spiritual muscles. Don't stop at the physical plane.
- Have a well-defined growth plan to maximize your strengths and minimize your weaknesses. As leadership expert John Maxwell says, "You must know yourself to grow yourself."
- Your rituals are for you. Other people will not understand

and you should not expect them too. As you see results you will lose the need for outside approval.

- Study your mastermind. Understand everyone's flaws as well as their strengths. Don't allow their weaknesses to become excuses for you rather let their humanity keep you humble.
- Remember specific qualities of each individual member of your mastermind that you want to emulate. Keep these qualities in front of you and practice them.
- Meet with your physical mastermind on a regular basis. Meditate using your mental mastermind.
- Keep God first and fall in love with the process.

Conclusion

Excellence looks good on you. You are a unique individual and once you begin to adopt a spirit of excellence, all your personal attributes that make you who you are, will shine. Excellence is like an ultra violet black light on your life that exposes every speck of greatness you are sprinkled with. It reveals things you didn't know were there and the exciting part is you will start noticing your glow growing brighter. When you finally walk in the awareness of who you are called to be, it's as if you are wearing all white under a black light. Your glow will be powerful unlike anyone else's. This can be confusing if you are not comfortable with who you are. What looked like greatness in the past is not necessarily your greatness. Embrace your uniqueness and love the skin you're in. You are the new exception to old rules.

Keep going. No matter what.

- *Reginald Lewis*

Chapter III - Black, Whole
The Exception Law
Don't let wealth escape you

Things aren't always what they seem. Wealth is silent.
The masses move in a predictable way. Reject the status quo and
embrace being different.

Staying in the Black

Your finance professionals (banker, advisor, CPA, Attorney)
should be just as, or more important to you, then your barber or
hair stylist. This is another one of those paradigm shifts. Your stylist
will dress up the "outside" but your banker pays more attention to
the "inside." If you haven't quite reached the O.G. - Obtaining
Greatness mindset, you will argue the benefit that looking good has
on your psyche. I challenge you to imagine what benefits true
financial freedom bring.

In 1966, a young man was born in Compton, California to
parents who imparted to him the spirit of entrepreneurship. From
an early age, John Hope Bryant would witness the disparity within
his community and not only ask why, but he wanted to make a
difference. Operation Hope, Inc. was founded in the aftermath of
the Rodney King riots in Los Angeles, California. Its mission is to
eradicate poverty through what Bryant calls a "Silver Rights
Movement." Operation Hope fosters financial literacy,
entrepreneurship, and access to capital to underserved communities
of color. Through various partnerships, Bryant has opened Hope
Inside offices in multiple banks, schools and community centers
across the country.

The power of financial literacy, to help eradicate poverty in our community, cannot be trivialized. You work hard but you spend harder. Spending became the drug that eases the edge of a hard life. I should ask, are you giving this drug to your kids?

When I was eight years old I opened my first passbook savings account. Every other Friday, I would gather my dollars and make my deposit. The bank was in my neighborhood a few blocks from where I lived. I remember walking up those brick steps and going into Second National Bank where Mrs. Odessa would take my dollars and deposit slip and give me my receipt. This was a big deal for me.

An even bigger deal was the manager of the bank was a man who looked just like me. Harry McBride was one of the few, if not the only, black men running a financial institution in my city. Every time I made a deposit, or withdrawal, Mr. McBride in true O.G. fashion would greet me with a "give me five," cool and dignified as only he could. If you watch how black men great each other or the elaborateness of our handshakes, you can tell the extent of our relationship. "Give me five" is empowering for a young African American boy from his banker. He attempted to connect with me and it worked.

My relationship with Harry grew into me having my own successful banking career. He was also one of the men I developed my sense of style from. He was an impeccable dresser. On your journey to O.G. - Obtaining Greatness mindset, there will always be someone who has reached O.G. status that is willing to pour into you. Stay away from those who appear to have arrived, but are unapproachable and unwilling to share what they know. There's a difference between leadership by position or title and a true servant leader. Harry McBride made a difference in the life of a young black boy in his community.

Financially Lit

When I was younger, my level of financial literacy was higher than most of my friends and family. Unfortunately for me, your life will likely emulate those closest around you. I know you have heard the saying the rich get richer and the poor get poorer. What makes this statement true is not some elaborate scheme although some would argue otherwise. There is a law of like attracts like.

Poverty is a mindset and poor people aren't always comfortable around wealth, and vice versa. The conversations are different and there is a different way of looking at life. An O.G. isn't comfortable hanging around those who are not trying to obtain common goals. It's not that any group is better than another, it goes back to education and learning the language. I'm not talking about your native tongue. I am talking about understanding finance. What is your money mindset? Depending on how you grew up, and your parent's relationship with money, you may have been preconditioned to spend every dollar you made. Now, most of our families were hard-working people, but sometimes our level of consumption was greater than or equal to whatever we produced.

This is not a recipe for greatness. When you are living paycheck to paycheck, you give up all your power and are enslaved to your job. Sometimes you will hear "job" described as a J.O.B. This stands for "just over broke." Let me say there is nothing wrong with a job. This is one of many options for making money. It's the most popular option among the masses but not so much in wealthy circles.

Follow these four steps to stay in the black:

1. Learn the language of finance. Can you imagine being in a foreign country and not knowing how to speak the language? If you can't speak the native tongue how limited would your opportunities be? Would you possibly get taken advantage of?

2. Stay out of debt. Never use debt on an asset that will not hold its value or appreciate.

3. Own your own business. Always bet on yourself before you take a chance on others. There is nothing wrong with working for someone else, but make this choice because you want to, not because you must.

4. Expand your horizon. Don't get caught up or limited by your small experiences. There is a lot more to life. Live it.

You might live in an environment that encourages the exact opposite to what was aforementioned. Remember, you are the "exception." The crowd will move one way, but the O.G. - Obtaining Greatness mindset causes you to move differently.

The Color Matrix

You derive a higher value from your difference than from your sameness. Meaning anything that sets you apart from the status quo is a plus. That is The Exception Law. Unfortunately, social pressures make it hard for us to understand this. No guy wants a girl who's just like all the other girls. But most girls are trying to "fit in" a common mold created by popular culture and current societal norms. Mediocre companies will "diversify" their workforce just for the optics of it and fail to harness the ingenuity, cultural competencies and social awareness that adds to the bottom line. My point is that "different" is great.

Different adds value. It distinguishes between what has been and the future. Different is innovative. It's what O.G. - Obtaining Greatness is now, relative to what we've known in the past. This is who you are; the one that doesn't think like everyone else. The one who was an outcast and not included within the cliques or, if you were involved in those circles, you knew you didn't really belong. You are that rarity that stands out and is noticed even if you don't want to be. Stop dimming your light. Shine bright. I know, I make it sound easy. How do you embrace your difference?

The Devil is a Liar

The world as we know it is not real. There's more to it than what we see with our natural eye and that's why many of us see varying levels of brightness. There is a way to find clarity and live our lives however we want to. This varies according to different perceptions. I call it the Color Matrix. If you remember the blockbuster "Matrix" movie trilogy you know what I'm talking about. The Color Matrix reveals what your personal reality is depending on which "pill" you decide to take. These special pills release a dye that runs through our veins and shows the condition of our heart. Most of the time the medicine you take hinders you from seeing any other way. Choose carefully.

The Red Pill

Here is the truth. These are the facts regardless of how ugly, how indicting, or how they personally paint you. Sometimes we don't want to deal with reality. Some would say you can't handle the truth. I wish most people would take the red pill. People do not understand how serious race relations are in America. When I say serious, I mean how close we are to reliving the early twentieth century.

Have you ever talked with someone who only sees from their point of view and have no desire to even attempt to look from another's point of view? There is zero empathy when it comes to the discussion of race in America. Until we change this we will be a backward nation.

As an O.G., you should always confront the truth. You never want to get to a place where you are fooling yourself. Unfortunately, very few of us know and understand this truth and even less desire to know. It's something you must experience. Red pill discussions can be very contentious and, without the strength of character, you can become very angry at the lack of humanity in the world. This pill should be taken with a full-strength "solution."

The White Pill

This is really a placebo. You think you have a catalyst for action but because of the inert rhetoric expressed by all concerned, nothing happens. The white pill is the "yes but" pill. You know those types who always have a "but" to every truth and will affirm or deny according to their argument. The people that accept slavery as a fact but then say, "at least they were clothed," or "some masters were very good to their slaves," these are white pill people. Don't confuse white pill people with white people. Black people can take this pill too. "Be quiet, at least it's not as bad as it once was." Or, I was oppressed so I have a right to_____ (fill in the blank). It's all talk. When you're under white pill influence, you want "rights" without "responsibilities." Accountability lacks across the board.

The Blue Pill

These are your deniers. Once you take the blue pill you go back to sleep and, if it's all right in your household, that's all that matters. Blue pill people accept things as they are. They accept the history books as they were written and are straight up status quo folks. These are not your critical thinkers or intellectuals or anyone who may be perceived as rocking the boat. When confronted with the reality of the red pill, most people opt out and take the blue pill. Your vision is limited to the visible spectrum only. There is no greatness for you. More jobs, less crime and the flavor of the day politics will satisfy you. Most politicians like blue pill people because they're easiest to control. Many don't even vote. Martin Luther King Jr. spoke about this pill when he said, "The only thing necessary for the triumph of evil is for good men to do nothing."

The Black Pill

This pill is strictly for those with the O.G. - Obtaining Greatness mindset. If you take the black pill, you will recognize all the hate, bigotry, unfairness, and the disadvantages of minorities. You see and you feel the daily struggle. You understand what it means to be black in America. And then…, you go out and do it anyway (it being whatever you want it to be). You determine if it was done before, surely you can do it again. Nothing can stop you.

When you take the black pill, your brain receives that moment of clarity that allows you to see what's inside and what's outside your "locus of control" or what you can readily do something about. If you can't control it, don't worry about it. This clarity will enable you to win the long game. You begin to understand each piece on the chessboard and what their abilities and limitations are. Once you take the black pill, you recognize haters are going to hate and you never acknowledge or speak to that fact again. It's another moot point not up for discussion.

Talking about your haters is like complaining about the weather. Don't waste your time. You also realize whoever is in power is not going to give up ANY of that power just because you asked nicely, or because you voted. The black pill causes you to recognize the importance of time; also, the influence of money. These two elements, when allowed to germinate, will lead to power. Have you ever been in a fruitless conversation? How much time do you allow these conversations to waste in your life? Measure your wealth, not only in dollars but, in time!

The black pill will cause you to become more of a producer and less of a consumer. When you take the black pill, you will begin to recognize concepts like equity and appreciating assets and real estate. This is a prescription that causes you to get more passport stamps. There are O.G.'s all around the world we haven't met yet. The black pill will stop you from just looking for a job; it opens your eyes to all types of opportunity.

There are side effects. Watch the drug interactions. You can't have hate in your heart if you decide to take the black pill. You will only partially benefit and you can't call yourself a true O.G. This tablet is the most expensive pill to swallow. Don't allow hate to have you pay the price for black and end up with a less potent, generic knockoff.

Hood Mentality

Mindset is like a roadmap we travel accordingly. Some maps have been distorted over time and, unfortunately, those navigating with these distorted maps have been ill-informed. They become gatekeepers to a psyche conscious men won't understand nor does it fit the greatness paradigm. The attitude is corrupt and the rituals are barbaric. This mastermind seems to seat Lucifer himself. This is different in the worst way because it lacks humanity. The "hood" contaminates what this great country is supposed to be. Even though it represents a small minority of America's citizens, I've had my encounters.

Always up for a good time, my cousin and a friend of ours decided to take a ride and enjoy the warm summer evening. We were all still in high school so summer for us was a time to let loose and embrace whatever came our way. Usually, it was those of the fairer sex. It was getting late and we decided to drive into an area we'd never been before. We came upon a stretch of street that seemed deserted except for some lights in the distance that we couldn't make out from where we were.

Being the young want-to-be tough guys we were, we investigated. As we approached the area, some of the lights appeared to be headlights surrounding what looked like… a bonfire? At 16, with a muted sense of mortality, we ignored an eerie feeling coming over us and went even closer. Like a moth to a flame about to be genuinely burned by a fire, we end up 20 yards from a Klan cross burning ceremony; hood, white sheets and all. You know how you see something and think it can't really be real? Not sensing the danger because of the unbelief of the situation, we froze in silence. Until someone yelled, "Get the hell out of here." Some not so common events in life aren't real to you unless you go through it personally. This was my first, but not the last experience with the Ku Klux Klan. Sometime later, they held a march through town in their more modern garb of a black uniform with swastika badges.

Hate in the form of a hood, or hate that is self-inflicted, has no place in an O.G. It takes too much energy. Take exception to hate. It limits you from growing and living the abundant life. If you give in to hate, you are stunted by someone or something you have no control over. What you believe can become your demise, or a self-fulfilling prophecy. O.G. - Obtaining Greatness is a different belief system. You must believe it for it to work for you.

Lack of confidence in the stability of a bank will cause a "bank run." A bank run happens when depositors lose confidence in the bank's ability to meet the demands of depositors and they all withdraw at the same time. The failure of the bank then comes from their belief or lack thereof. So, an otherwise stable, sound and solvent institution can fail because of the very actions of those with a stake in the organization. It's in your best interest to drop the hate or you will succumb to it. Have faith in the value of your community or there will be a "run" on it.

The Wealth of the Wicked

According to the Scriptures, "The wealth of the wicked is laid up for the just." You might take this passage of scripture to mean you will inherit wealth one day in the sweet "bye and bye" without hard work and diligence. Some of us, to be spiritual, just want to be lucky. And even with a carnal concept like luck, the agnostic knows, "the harder I work, the luckier I get." When we say wicked, we are talking about an unjust system.

Anything which is founded on deception, cheating or anything which goes against principal is not sustainable in the long run. You may attempt to get wealth by unscrupulous means, but the Exception Law will not work on that plane. You will get caught. The game is changing, and power is shifting back to the people. You have the convenience and the mobility to live work or play anywhere in the world.

We must change the way we traditionally look at work. There has to be a redistribution of where we spend our income and where that income comes from. As I said before, there is nothing wrong with that corporate job. But, I challenge you to understand that that is not the only way. Are you the one in your family that everyone comes to for advice? Are all your friends calling you on the phone for relationship help? You may make a great life coach. Don't fret because there is no one around you doing that kind of job. It could be a need you're able to fulfill. That's where The Exception Law kicks in. There are a lot of life coaches that are living their dreams. Are you the one who always caters the events? Do you have that artistic eye and a way with colors and details? Then you may be a great event planner. There are many areas that you may have expertise in and there are many ways to capitalize on that expertise. You will need to change your view on jobs and how to make a living. You will need to take some risk. Recognize that this is a different mindset than most are used to. But how do you condone betting on your boss before you bet on yourself? This should inspire you to get serious about your growth game. One thing about God, if you have the faith to take one step, He will always take two. This is what the, "wealth of the wicked," means to me. Doubt and unbelief are holding your wealth!

How many times have you seen other people who are far less talented than you excel in an endeavor only because they had the faith to try and you didn't? It's difficult to wear the title "man or woman of faith" and behave like this. When there is incongruence between our spirit and what we are physically doing day-to-day it causes massive amounts of stress. Not only is this stressful for us, but these are the actions we are teaching our children.

Generations ago it was expected kids would work. There was no question about it. This is what you did after school, you worked; in the field or factory. The next generation, the expectation was you would go to college. There was no question about it. The hope was, go to school, graduate, and get a good job. But do you know the conversation at some breakfast tables is that you will never work for anyone, but you will have your own? Or, you will work for the experience then come home to run the family business. That failure, risk, and playing big is just a part of life if you want to reap great rewards. These are "great" lessons. What would you do if you were not afraid to fail?

You are different in a significant way. Your beauty is in your difference. Your creativity is in your difference. Your greatness will be in your difference. You may have been beaten down and judged harshly because of your differences, but your differences have made you very resilient. O.G. equals resiliency. It's in your blood, it's in your DNA, it is what makes you great.

Risk Management

I never lend money to family. Some people may see this as harsh and greedy, especially family, but this is critical. This is my way to keep our relationships from going south. This doesn't mean I'm not generous, it's just I will prefer giving then lending; when it comes to family. This is a guard against unmet expectations. I've even had family pay me back anyway, but that's not an expectation.

When you are investing you expect a return on what you funded. That can mean your money, time or other resources directed in an endeavor. Never take more losses than you can afford. You will take losses, however, just make sure what you're risking provides an adequate probability of reward. This is the difference between investing and gambling. A gambler will fall prey to all kinds of fallacies and probability will not be in his favor. Hence, the house always wins.

... Wilt thou be made whole?

- John 5:6

One difference between "good" and "great," a "G" and an "O.G.," is the size of the bets being placed and if you are accredited to play on this playing field. Stay with me, I'm going to get you there.

Black Billions

One of my favorite autobiographies was written by the late Wall Street attorney Reginald Lewis, "Why Should White Guys Have All the Fun?" This is the story of Lewis's impact on Wall Street during the eighties. Lewis was a corporate attorney and his story is very inspirational. In the late eighties, Lewis organized and executed the billion-dollar takeover of Beatrice International, the giant food conglomerate. This was the first takeover of this magnitude orchestrated by an African American.

I remember following some of Lewis's business acquisitions when they were highlighted in the *Wall Street Journal* or on the evening news. Lewis was born in Baltimore, Maryland to a middle-class family who instilled in him O.G. - Obtaining Greatness principles. Although she didn't reference these principles the way this book does, it was Lewis's grandmother who taught him to be sure to keep a piece of everything he earned. This meant to save your money and don't live broke.

Throughout school Reginald Lewis excelled academically and in sports. After graduating from Virginia State University, he attended Harvard Law school. It was here Lewis learned the "language." Corporate law fascinated Lewis and he knew he had to be in on the deal-making. One of his early successes was the purchase of the company McCall Pattern. This was a pattern maker which had a dominant market share in its industry. This significant deal wet Lewis's palette and prepared him for greater acquisitions to come. When the opportunity to buy Beatrice International came about, Lewis had already cut his teeth. He was ready and nothing would stop him. Although Lewis died at the young age of 50, his legacy continues through the many philanthropic contributions he made over his lifetime and continues to make today.

In the black community, because of the many past and present injustices, we are stuck playing defense on every play. Sometimes (and I stress the "sometimes") this is a matter of life and death. Mostly, I believe this is learned behavior. If you are stuck playing not to lose, you seldom win big. At most, you break even. This is by default because of the defensive thought process.

Everyone that has anything, including money, freedom, and happiness, plays offense. Being one man playing offense doesn't win in the long run. You need a team, a community. The identity crisis in our community stops us from having a great offense whenever we play team ball. There's ten seconds left on the clock and you are being triple teamed; somebody is open.

Black I.C.E.

Diseases like Alzheimer's or dementia which affect the brain are horrible for the individual suffering and those charged to provide care, namely family members. ALS is a debilitating neurological disease that affects muscle movement. Also, known as Lou Gehrig disease for baseball great Lou Gehrig, funding for a cure is crucial for those facing this emergency. A fundraising challenge which went viral raised millions of dollars for treatment. It was called the Ice Bucket Challenge. You may recall many online videos depicting a person surrounded by friends, family or colleagues standing or sitting as a bucket of ice water was poured over their heads. For some people, this is fun, and it brings awareness to those suffering from this dreaded disease. Although I didn't subject myself to this humiliation, I have donated to the cause.

There's an emergency in the black community. It is a disease that comes from a lack of understanding how a dollar circulates and the significance of increasing circulation through more black hands. Much of this problem is structural. Underdeveloped communities don't provide all the products and services needed. When this happens, people don't shop in their communities which leads to more underdevelopment. You can see the problem. Black communities must embrace vertical integration (We will discuss owning the means of production).

69

This disease is partly psychological. This problem has plagued the black community for a long time. When I was a child, there was a saying that black people had been so brainwashed they believed white people's ice water was colder. This is an emergency. The problem is evident. I know without a doubt "Jim" over across the tracks doesn't like me. It's a much more profound realization when I understand I don't really like myself. Voting against your best interest is no different from conducting business the same.

People and businesses, that you choose to spend your money with, don't care about your community if _you_ don't care about your community. This may sound harsh as you read it, but it makes perfect sense. I don't care how I drive a rental car, but I treat my own vehicle with delicate care. This doesn't make me a bad person (you always hear this), I just don't have a vested interest beyond the rental rate. Nor does Walmart have a vested interest beyond the product it provides you (maybe they should).

This changes when there's ownership. "Buy back the block" is a very catchy phrase, but if there are no financial resources behind it, it will fall on deaf ears after a while. Again, this is an emergency, and we must believe our water is "colder" or at least as "cold" as any other water. _We_ must make our water drinkable again. I hope you understand no one will do it for you. This is Exception Law thinking; the masses continue waiting.

Blacker Berries

In 2008, the United States elected its first black president. Barack Hussain Obama became the 44th president of the United States of America. This was a very significant milestone for many reasons. I remember reminiscing on how far our country had come to reach this point. Although there were racial challenges, everyone felt the United States had turned a page on its ugly past.

We know what the aftermath was and without going into detail, I think we can agree President Obama had his work cut out for him. This president was exceptional in many ways. As the leader of the free world, his steps were meticulous. What can we learn from this? You and I are far removed from the duties of this great man, and yet, the slightest offense can send us from zero to 100 faster than a European sports car. This is the lesson. Thick skin and self-control is a sign of an O.G. Barack Obama was an O.G.

Master communicators will always leave the opposition name calling because it's all the opposition has left in their arsenal and an O.G. will not participate. What I thought was a page being turned was a mirror being lifted to America so she could see her true self. Many people don't believe the reflection they see, and yet they participate daily in this authentic reality.

Whether you like it or not, Barack Obama is who we are. As I say this, I know the detractors will point out everything negative. I stand here before you and I point out everything great. But, even the negatives that have been attributed to this great man are a stretch, to say the least. You heard me say this before. The "greatness" in me will always recognize the "greatness" in you. If I can never find any greatness in anyone, that is very telling.

Our current president (at the time of this writing) Donald J. Trump, is a great politician. Before your mind instinctively floods with negative thoughts and feelings, stay with me. I may have lost a portion of my audience, but please, keep reading. The same thing we do with President Obama, seeing only what we choose to, is the same thing we do with President Trump. For the record, I did not vote for him.

Leadership can be summed up in one word, influence. Liking me is secondary, if necessary at all. I didn't bring up our current president to honor him but to make a point. There are times when the end justifies the means. He won. We want to win. I am not saying be like President Trump. What I am saying is there must be something inside of his playbook I can benefit from. There is some good in the worst of us and some bad in the best of us.

An O.G. has a degree of objectivity when he approaches any situation. In other words, stop being so emotional. President Obama understood this and he also knew what to say and when to say it. In the face of blatant disrespect, he was always calm, cool and collected. Is there a time to speak your mind? Absolutely! The question is, did you get the desired results? Go back a month, six months even one year and analyze the action taken versus the results achieved. Most of the time the results obtained, at most is it, "made us feel good" or "we got it off our chest or I gave him a piece of my mind." If you want to experience the O.G. - Obtain Greatness lifestyle all of that has got to go. Remember, this is chess not checkers. When faced with an emergency, remember who you are.

O.G. Code - Bet on Black

You are fearfully and wonderfully made. There is nothing wrong with you. Most of your opposition will be from people who wish to have your unique qualities, attributes and yes, even color. The Exception Law allows you to understand that just because it's always been doesn't mean it will continue to be. Give yourself a pass if you make a mistake. Forgive yourself. You must decide what comes next. O.G., you don't fit the status quo and you never will. You are a one of a kind original; the exception to the worldly rule. Use the following to capitalize on your difference.

- Embrace your creativity. You have a unique style and way of doing it. Don't allow it to be squashed or diminished because someone else doesn't understand.

- When what you feel is contrary to what's around you, go with your gut. Never allow intuition to fade behind the noise of the crowd.
- Cultivate your gift. Your creativity is a broad expression of your possibilities, but your "gift" is uniquely you. It is what you do best. It may not be what you get paid to do currently but don't let that stop you.
- Embrace your "black sheep" status. The sooner you do, the sooner you are relieved of the pressure of trying to please people who will never accept anything but the "old" you.
- Don't let your past take hostage of your future. Live in the right now and do what you can today. If you do this, tomorrow will take care of itself.
- Accept your right-ness, righteousness, and perfection. Only the great will recognize greatness in others. The opposite is also true. The miserable will see it everywhere they look.
- The wisdom of crowds is not for you. Watch crowds and understand how you can profit from them. Step out of the picture long enough to recognize the trends. If you want to be a trendsetter, understand first mover advantage.
- Never let anyone shake your resolve. Most of us allow our buttons to be pushed too quickly. Thus, we hand over control to our adversary. When you think of what your ancestors endured, surely you can bite your tongue for strategy's sake. For the long game. This is chess.

Conclusion

Out of the night that covers me
Black as the pit from pole to pole
I thank whatever gods may be
For my unconquerable soul.

This is a line from a poem by William Ernest Henley. Your differences make you unique and should be used as a competitive advantage. You are forged from material unlike any other. It's a superior material because it could not be destroyed under the worst circumstances. It could not be conquered. The masses are the same, and that makes them extremely predictable while you are incredibly mobile and unpredictable. This is a blessing and a curse.

It is a blessing because you can move at the drop of a hat and turn on a dime. You think differently. You talk differently and you walk differently. You were made "Whole," accept that. Everything about you is what others want to be. You are blessed. The curse comes from believing in and spending all your energy attempting to assimilate with the masses. Forget what everyone else is doing, find your niche and master it. When you add blackness on top of your excellence and mastery on top of your blackness you will see greatness. In the next chapter, we will expand on your niche and how it enhances your greatness.

I find freedom sexy. I find freedom so sexy, I can't even explain it to you. You wake up every day and feel like you can do anything.

— *Prince*

Chapter IV - That O.G. Thing
The Intensity Law
One dream at a time

Something great happens whenever you give your undivided attention to a task. If you do many things at once, it's never your best work. Focus!

Be In it to Win it

To reach the level of greatness you are pursuing, the O.G. - Obtaining Greatness level, you will need these three elements; passion, intensity and momentum. If you lack one, your success will resemble a three-legged stool where one leg is shorter than the others, or has broken off completely. You are not optimized for stability and the risk of taking a fall increases. Divide this instability across many unrelated projects and you are headed toward failure.

"Good" is the enemy to "great" when you are on your journey to O.G. - Obtaining Greatness. How many good things in your life are holding you back from that great or "that O.G. thing?" What is that O.G. thing? It's the one thing in your life right now that if you would stop, focus and complete it, would change your life. This is often hard to recognize because as a society, we have embraced multitasking to the extent we are never fully engaged. We lack in quality, excellence, and depth. How can you really be great at everything or even many things if they're not somehow related?

Serial Entrepreneur

Growing up in the family business taught me many valuable lessons. We were vertically integrated. There was the real estate business. We rented space to residents, small office, beauty salons

76

and barber shops. Some of the businesses we rented to were family owned. The commercial real estate space also included storage, a supply store and banquet facility. Retail apparel and haircare products were sold to salon and barber clients and professional products were sold to the hair care professionals who rented from us. You could come get your hair styled or cut, grab all your hair maintenance products, an outfit, and come back later that night to party in the banquet facility. This didn't happen overnight. It started in a basement, with a truck. It grew incrementally from there. I like the way the author of "Rich Dad Poor Dad" Robert Kiyosaki puts it. He uses an acronym, F.O.C.U.S. "Follow one course until successful." Scripture says that a double-minded man is unstable in all his ways. You don't even have to be a Believer to recognize the truth in that statement. How do we get laser-like focus to masterfully complete one project at a time and grow successfully? Let's find out.

Jack of All Trades

Ever since I was a kid I wanted to work in the financial markets. I found it fascinating how wealth was created, managed and transferred, sometimes destroyed. I understood the stock market and real estate market were partly responsible for the disparity between the haves and the have not's. Most of us will participate in real estate if only purchasing our primary residence; maybe additional rental property. But there's not enough of us on the other side of the wealth gap participating in the financial markets.

I had a goal of becoming a stockbroker but, if I was honest with myself, that type of action was not happening in Saginaw, Michigan, where I lived. If it did, it would not be on the level of New York or Chicago or Philadelphia. As much as I love my hometown, we were small potatoes and I had little chance of making it if I stayed there. It was like saying you want to be a famous actor but you're not willing to move to New York or Los Angeles. Note that I came up in the pre-internet days when proximity meant a lot. Later, I realized this was a part of my holding pattern and I still needed to work some things out. I did complete my Master of Business Administration (MBA) degree, which was good. I started a banking job locally, that was good. I also completed other credentials, that was good, too. Notice nothing great was happening?

I want you to stop and think about all the "good" things in your life that prevented you from being "great." Did you get married? Did you have kids? Did you start a job that paid just enough to keep you satisfied? Did you buy a lot of stuff you are still paying off? That's not good, but it will have you delusional and out of touch with the greatness within. Think about it. You may drive a nice car and live in a decent home, and the areas I mentioned above provide you a degree of satisfaction, but it's still the status quo (yes you can be great married with children; understand what season you're in).

My last job was Director of Trading for a local bank. I don't want to make this sound like I made it to my dream. The title afforded me very little concerning market exposure. We were a very conservative shop. Most of our wealthy clients were wealthy before they got to us so I was just managing the store. If nothing happened and there was no excitement I was doing a good job. It was not "great," just "good." This is how I knew I was in the wrong place. Everything was good and it was too status quo. It was not O.G. and I couldn't use my gifts and talents effectively. In fact, those last few years, I probably regressed. If you don't focus in on your O.G. thing, greatness will elude you as well. The perceived security of my job, and the title which really had nothing to do with my passions, stopped me from going further. I rationalized that it was close to what I wanted. That O.G. thing caused me to take another step forward and not settle.

New Jack

Multi-tasking has been taunted as the must-have skill you put on your resume. Knowing how to shuffle between tasks, balancing and completing on time. Continuing to do more with less. Do you believe you do your best work when you're simultaneously working on multiple projects? If you answered yes, I would challenge you to consider changing your mindset.

I agree with the consensus that when we can multi-task, we may increase the efficiency of our workload. You may be able to process more volume but it will hardly be your best work. Studies have shown how distracted work has more mistakes and is seldom the quality of a person who's dedicated to one project.

You really should consider changing the way you think on this one and I know I won't convince a lot of you. It's like that drunk uncle who swears he's a better driver when he's intoxicated. He may make it home but it's more luck than skill. There are unimportant tasks where "good" is good enough. You can multi-task these if you want (finished is better than perfect). Again, we want to be "great" not "good."

I used to read at least one book per week and I had a goal of making it to a book every few days! I read about these leaders that are so efficient with their reading schedules. The amount of information was mind-boggling. I have learned, for me personally, depth is far better than quantity.

I have an extensive library. I have given away over half of it throughout my life. What I realized is wisdom is gained if you take a book and learn the material. Sure, all of it may not be for you, but

79

there is a wealth of knowledge to be had in a single book. I don't believe we scratch the surface in one week not to mention a day.

Some may argue a lot of non-fiction is saying what past authors have said. I think that shows the value in sitting with an author and letting it marinate for a while. Everyone has unique experiences some of them just like yours. When you connect on a personal level you gain even more from the reading experience and the book delivers even deeper value.

This requires a new level of focus many of us are not ready for. Society will have you continue gaining greater efficiencies as incremental value added decreases, or becomes negative. The O.G. is looking to increase his effectiveness as well. Relationships are another one of those areas where we don't like to put the time in and we struggle to understand why people don't just see things our way. To be effective with people you must take the time and, for everything else, sometimes less is more.

There is no intensity without consistency

The intensity law tells us we need laser-like focus. That O.G. thing becomes what we are shooting for and, to hit our target, we must be consistent in our actions. When you take up arms you are at war but the first battle is with yourself. What stops you from being consistent?

Fatal distractions

It is 5 o'clock in the morning and I am still writing to meet yesterday's deadline. My sump pump needed replacing and, instead of calling a plumber, I did not value my time. I was "penny wise and pound foolish." Six hours after I started and two trips to the hardware store, I'm finished! Things like these are distractions. They're only fatal when you allow enough of them to disrupt your rituals. Many things in life can be fatal but they don't kill right away.

As you look at the distractions in your life, are you able to tell which ones are fatal? Are you ready to tell the difference between necessary diversions and unnecessary distractions? Distractions keep you from being consistent. It's rarely the same distraction that knocks you off course. There should be a level of commitment on your part that puts your O.G. thing ahead of anything else. This can be very difficult considering most people will not understand greatness or what it takes to be great.

The world has long since become satisfied with average, or less. Not even good but just plain old average. Most of the time, distractions creep in when we do not have our rituals in order. Or, when we have not had the routine in place consistently to teach those around us the value of and the need to protect our time.

Distractions destroy your momentum. Have you ever started a new diet plan before getting rid of all the food you're not supposed to eat? Sometimes, this is food that will be consumed by other family members. Even so, to you, it is a distraction. Willpower alone will not allow you to overcome that distraction and soon enough that diet is on the back burner. You did not have enough time put into the consistency that would give you the momentum. You didn't start with enough intensity. When we do something intensely we engulf ourselves in it. It becomes a part of who we are.

This is not a problem if we only focus on one thing at a time. Once we have accomplished the task at hand, we can move on to something else. If there are other obligations, for example, family, community or personal downtime, scheduling that into our rituals allows us to continue building intensity. Here are five key ways to keep distractions from becoming fatal and keep the Intensity Law working in your favor.

1. Educate the people around you.

If most of the people you do business with know you only check email twice a day once in the morning and once late afternoon, you are free from distracting emails that enter your inbox all times of the day. Most of the time, there's nothing that couldn't wait a few hours anyway. This works well at home with your family, too.

2. Schedule in downtime.

You will feel like you don't need it. Don't work to the point your body makes you rest. Watch the signals your body gives you and respond accordingly. You are not a machine. Your humanity will get in the way of you executing correctly if you don't do the preventative maintenance.

3. Use a timer.

There is a technique called the Pomodoro method. It allows you to time your movements and time your breaks from work. You are committed to a block of time, for example, 20 or 30 minutes. At the end of the block of time you can reward yourself by checking email, getting a snack or stretching. This method is beneficial for many people who struggle with procrastination.

4. Monitor the areas of your life where distractions are reoccurring.

The frequency of the same disturbance may point to an area in your life that needs to be investigated. What is happening that gets swept under the rug or has become the norm?

5. Don't let monsters continue to grow up.

If something deserves your attention, correct it while it's small and not a problem.

Practiced concentration

I attended a yoga class one day and, for the life of me, I could not follow along. I was intensely focused then suddenly I had to go the bathroom. But after I went and came back, the feeling of anxiousness and the total lack of concentration continued. We live in an over-stimulated world where parents and children are lacking the necessary focus. The average length of a song played on the radio is 3 to 4 minutes. This is because we can't focus any longer than that. Between texting, tweeting, snapping and posting there is no meaningful conversation or dialogue. Concentrate on what's being said, or not said. This sheds light on our listening habits or the lack thereof. Most of the time, instead of listening, we are getting together our arguments so we can be heard too. Concentrated listening comes from a sincere desire to understand what the other person is trying to say. At this point, you are having a conversation and not just attempting to talk.

Listening intensely

The Intensity Law affects your personal life, too. Are you listening or are you just hearing? There is a difference you know. One is mechanical and the other is relational. Can you guess which is which? For you to change your mindset and see a different perspective, listening is crucial. The O.G. - Obtaining Greatness method of listening requires us to be able to not only listen to what's being said but to take responsibility for making sure we understand what is being communicated.

This can be challenging to do because everyone wants to get their point across. It goes something like this. I listen to what you're saying to me. I'm entirely focused and not getting my conversation ready in my head to talk back. Once I hear you out and I have allowed you to say everything that you need to say, I repeat back to you in my own words to make sure I understood you. Then I ask, "Is this correct?" If it is not correct, I asked for clarification and repeat the process. If it is correct, then I can proceed with allowing you the opportunity to understand me.

There is power in allowing another person to be and to feel understood. The O.G. capitalizes on that power. It takes a lot of discipline, self-control and emotional confidence to do this. It is worth it in the end. You will see drastic changes in your life when you complete difficult tasks.

Larry, Curly and Big Mo

When I was 14 years old I was bullied. There were three kids and, to protect the not so innocent, let's call them Larry, Curly, and the big kid was Mo. During those days bullying was a lot different. We didn't have social media or cell phones to inflict pain on each other. Every day after school I had to make it from my seventh-hour class to the bus without running into these guys. While Larry and Curly caused me the most trouble, Mo was the ringleader. If you have ever found yourself in a situation dealing with people who did not like you and made it their goal to cause you pain, then you can imagine what I was going through.

During that time in my community, we would hurl insults at one another or "cap" on each other. Our parents called it "playing the dozens." There were a lot of "yo mama..." jokes involved. One day I got tired of Mo capping on me, partly because he was good at it. He could bring tears to a victim's eyes with his verbal assaults. I had enough and Mo was getting on my last nerve. After school, before I knew it I had taken my fist and I hit Mo straight in the face. There was a teacher nearby and we were broken up before there was really a fight. After that something happened. Those guys steered clear of me. I have since found that when you hit the biggest guy first the others will take notice and back down. The O.G. will always go for Mo.

If it's your job to eat a frog, it is best to do it first thing in the morning. If it's your job to eat two frogs, it is best to eat the biggest frog first. - *Mark Twain*

Something else happens when you take on tough challenges. The challenges after that seem more manageable. Mo was the leader of the group and I was wasting all my time worrying about Larry and Curly. When you are in the boardroom or a sales presentation do you know who the decision maker is? Taking the time to understand who's who will allow you to speed things up a bit; the Intensity Law is working in your favor. As you begin to move in the right direction momentum starts to increase.

Forward movement is a factor that will influence your staying power. If you spread yourself too thin, and in many directions, you will never gain momentum. This increases the probability that you will burn out. Hitting the "Big Mo," momentum allows you to do more than what you're able to do without it. I could not beat those three guys if I had to fight each one of them one on one. But I can beat all of them by hitting one of them. The right one. That is the Intensity Law.

Meaningful specific, or wandering generality

When was the last time you pissed somebody off? No, really? If you expect to be great, plan to piss people off. This does not mean that you're going to be a jerk with everyone. But it does say that there are some people and situations you don't have time for. When

I was in corporate America, I sometimes shut the door to my office to get my job done. I had colleagues that wanted to stop by and chat for a while and they are not very good at taking clues. I find when I shut my door not only is it quieter but I have fewer distractions. But then everyone wondered, "Why is Andre's door shut?" I would respectfully and politely answer any concerns and I kept my door shut. I was not paid to chit chat. If you're working for a company and you get fired because your door is shut, then it is not the company for you.

Do whatever it takes. Develop a habit of taking what's yours (your time). This gives you momentum toward what you desire. No one is going to give it to you. The best in our communities have performed "good" defense while others have practiced "intense" offense. Focus on that O.G. thing. This is your path to greatness.

Entrepreneurs, by nature, can have a tough time focusing on one project. They may have a grand idea but struggle with the details. They put time into their business and unfortunately lose interest before the company can carry itself. If you do this a couple more times your energies dissipate and time will get away from you. A concentrated effort in one of your ideas would have brought massive success. You are 20 years into your conglomerate of various designs with no sign of rest. None of your operations run successfully without you. When you start your business have an exit strategy. If you don't you risk your legacy, or you will be working a glamorized job unable to ever step away.

Some small businesses struggle with succession planning because the next generation wants none of this. They have seen it from the inside. The O.G. - Obtaining Greatness entrepreneur has a different way of looking at entrepreneurship. When you do start a business, there should come a time where that business is able to operate without your presence. Think in terms of systems, processes and procedures. Because we all know initially the entrepreneur will work far more hours than the employee. At some point, you want your time to be recouped. Also, ask yourself how many meaningful jobs are you creating for your community. Initially, you may only be able to provide pocket change or a supplement to someone else's full-time employment. Set your sights on significance. Ask yourself, "How can I provide a living wage?" What goals should this company set for revenue, to provide sustainable employment for those who have made the commitment to you? These goals may seem a little bit lofty but they are by no means beyond reach if you focus intensely. We want to get beyond paying under the table, needing to be there every day, and any other part where you are only halfway legit. In other words, have a business plan and stick to it. I think it was Zig Ziglar who said, "You cannot make it as a wandering generality, you must become a meaningful specific."

O.G. Code - I.F. Only... (Intense Focus)

The Intensity Law allows you to focus your energy on one thing, master it and then move to something else. This level of mastery is what O.G. - Obtaining Greatness living requires. It is an area where many entrepreneurs struggle. If you've noticed your attention span waning, The Intensity Law will keep you on track.

- Develop a routine and stick to it. It doesn't need to be elaborate. You want to make it easily accomplished so that as you stack these quick successes you form a habit you will want to continue.
- Meditate. Meditation will train you to slow your mind and allow you to regain control. Start your day in this state so it will carry over through your most productive activities.

- Read to learn, learn to master. Go deep instead of broad. Those one hundred books you read a year won't matter if you can't remember any of it.

- Define your audience or market then zero in specifically on who you want to work with. You may feel the need to serve and you may think that the broader the audience the better. Understand, if you are speaking to everyone you are focused on no one.

- Don't allow bad customers to soak up all your time. Know when to fold them. The customer is not always right and you eliminate a lot of headaches when you work with whom you want to work with. Sometimes it is better to cut them off.

- Know your calling. Watch out for passionfruit that changes with the seasons.

- Don't allow trivial things to break your focus. There will always be a distraction or a fire that needs putting out, but it doesn't always have to be put out by you. Know what is worthy of your attention.

- Train the people around you. Make time for yourself and time for your business. Don't allow any and everything to invade those times not even your loved ones. Once you have stood firm a few times, they will understand it is for the greater good and they will respect you for sticking to that O.G. thing.

- Be confident and focused on your idea but don't be rigid in your approach. Flexibility allows you to roll with the punches.

- Remember your mental game must be stronger than your physical game. This is not an excuse for laziness. Hard work will need to get done. Make sure it's the right work. Grow to where you work "on" your business not just "in" your business.

Conclusion

When an archer shoots an arrow with his bow, the angle of the trajectory will be dependent on how far he wants it to travel. If the prey is close enough, short and quick will get the job done. When the target is further out, drag and friction will hinder the arrow and he will need to adjust accordingly. It takes more skill to hunt long range but you're prepared. You were made for this and every success is remembered by the very fiber the makes up your muscle and nervous system. Believe in your ability.

In the next chapter, you'll learn The Release Law. It is the final component we will use to complete renovation on the inner man. Then we will direct our influence on those we are connected to or, "Your Crew." When you think about giving, you usually think of the benefit that will come to the receiver. This is especially true when it comes to forgiveness. But we will see this is more beneficial to the one doing the giving than to the receiver. This is still about you and this secret weapon will enable you to unlock power you did not know was accessible. But remember, you can't tap into this power with an old mindset. This far in, you should see some change taking place in what and how you chose to think. Keep your mind open for this next one. It's powerful!

It's not the load that breaks you down, it's the way you carry it.

– *Lena Horne*

Chapter V - Go Giver
The Release Law
You are blessed to be a blessing

Energy is neither created or destroyed. Allow life to flow through you. It's difficult to give on the level you were designed to if you are burdened with a heavy load.

Sacrifice

Have you ever learned something in life that changed some of your long-held beliefs? Our beliefs are entrenched in our lives and new information is not allowed in. Self-preservation is a basic instinct. While some could argue that this is the greatest instinct, this instinct is overwritten when something we love is in danger, for example, our children. We will die to save our children. What about a spouse? Would you risk your life for a dear friend? Have you ever considered what goes through the mind of a fireman when he rushes into a burning building? When there is a goal to reach, a new mindset is adopted to destroy the fears that have previously kept you from going forward. The "stuff" we hold onto is usually an old mindset, not O.G. - Obtaining Greatness.

Get Yours

No matter how much despair you experience in your life you can bless someone. You will always find someone worse off than you. If you look closely, your life is put into perspective as you open your heart to emphatically see the needs of others. This thought process changes your mindset of lack, to a mentality of abundance.

Poverty is an affliction of the mind as well as the bank account. I believe it's more of the former than the latter here in America. You don't know poverty until you travel the world. Poor people in America are some of the biggest consumers of "wants" versus "needs," relative to income. What is a "want" and what is a "need" can be debated. The obvious thing to do most times is to take care of yourself and most of us buy into this without a second thought. But, when it's time to put someone else before you, that's where the problem comes in.

When I was a kid I listened to a rap song called "Gotta Get Mine." This rap was a duet with Flint, Michigan native, M.C. Breed, and the great Tupac Shakur. They were both doing what they needed to do to "get theirs." This was a great song and, the funny thing is, it was a collaboration. Each artist benefited from the others skillset and audience. I challenge you to believe that for you to "get yours," help someone else "get theirs." I understand how illogical this sounds, but there is a law in play here that I call The Release Law.

Mindset playing tricks on me

Before we can learn to operate this law, it is essential to understand how we think. If we believe there is not enough to go around and, your gain must be someone else's loss, then you can understand the need to hold on to everything you have. Life becomes a zero-sum game. I got to get mine and you have to get yours. It's a competition. Or, you may believe that there is this unlimited supply of everything you need. There is enough for all and everyone can drink of this "well that never runs dry." My gain is not your loss. I'm a finance guy and I know you're asking, "How can this be? Numbers don't lie. If there are two opportunities and you take both, what's left for me?"

Economics is the study of how we use limited resources for our unlimited wants. For many years, the caveat to this was that we are rational creatures and we make sound decisions. We now know we don't always do what's in our perceived best interest and we aren't rational all the time. This is not a bad thing, just an observation to provide context to long held beliefs. Feeling and emotion play a part in our decisions.

Greed and fear are two of the strongest emotions we encounter. You may have what some call a "fixed" or scarcity mindset or, what others call a "growth," or an abundance mindset. If you are scarcity-minded, you believe there is not enough and you see life from this perspective. This could cause you to move with extreme care, or you are paralyzed with fear. Everything could be going great in your life, but you are confident the next calamity is right around the corner. This can become a self-fulfilling prophecy as you draw you same negative energy you put out.

If your mindset is set to abundance, the sky is the limit. This is the Release Law. This is very freeing because no matter what the situation is in your life, you become solution focused instead of problem focused. This puts you in a very resourceful state and, this too, can become a self-fulfilling prophecy.

Which scenario would you like to have operate in your life? O.G. - Obtaining Greatness is not in short supply. I read that a mother will continue to produce milk for her baby as long as there is a need, or if the baby places a demand on the mother. If you put a claim on your greatness within you will begin manifesting the qualities and attributes of this lifestyle. There will be no limits.

Demand Deposits

When you are operating under the Release Law it's not difficult to pour into other people. In fact, you recognize it's vital that you do. This is akin to the Holding Law. Your funds have been "released." Your time of delay is shortened and you can go forward to the next destination. Make sure you have a valid account on file that has sufficient funds to clear the transaction. Sometimes people do last minute good deeds to shortcut the process, but it doesn't work this way. You forgot about the five business day "hold."

Operating under this law is for those of you who are seasoned. In other words, if you have made sufficient deposits, you won't run the risk of overdrawing the account. When you need to write the check, the money is there. This level of liquidity allows you to operate in areas that would otherwise be off limits to you. This gives you prime position to transact with greatness. It's the extra that you receive or, that operates on your behalf, that you seemingly have nothing to do with. This is deceptive because those deposits were made over time and they have become the lubricant for you to move in life with less friction.

Self-Serve

The Release Law gives you the ability to operate in O.G. - Obtaining Greatness. This happens indirectly because it is in proportion to your level of service. I heard someone once say service is the rent you pay to be on earth. The correlation of what you do for others to your level of greatness will rise, disproportionately at first, then exponentially later. This goes far beyond dollars and cents. A selfish leader is an oxymoron. Don't concern yourself with what's released to you now. Understand an even greater release comes into your life later. Also, if you are looking out for your interest by sowing seeds now for later, it will be worth it. I hope it will be something you do from the heart.

O.G. - Obtaining Greatness is not something that can be manipulated or worked to your favor. It's hard work. It's service. It's a sacrifice. Everywhere you go, when you show up, things should get better. The environment should be a bit more enjoyable. The air is a little fresher. You are not a thermometer to only read the temperature. You are a thermostat that sets the temperature. Look for the reason you are where you are. There is a problem you are called to solve. Giving will increase your awareness and ability. You are looking for problems to solve.

Remember, always add value

What's your elevator pitch? An elevator pitch is when you have, at your disposal, a short conversation/presentation to convey what you do and how you can benefit the person you're engaging. Typically, quick enough to deliver within the average time for an elevator ride. Have you ever run into someone influential and could have participated in a mutually beneficial conversation but you were not focused? You didn't have your thoughts together. After they were gone you remembered everything you wanted to say. It's not what they can do for you, but what you can do for them.

The most important part of your pitch is your value proposition. What do you bring to the table? What's in it for them? In other words, how are you going to increase their life? This is how you want to engage people. Notice, I didn't say, "Important people." I know you may be thinking, "You seriously want me to walk around pouring into everyone else making sure they're good? What about me?" That is exactly what I want you to do! See, they're "good," you're O.G. - Obtaining Greatness! Ask yourself, "What's your value add?"

Unfortunately, I can't look at all the good deeds you've done in the past. That's water under the bridge, as my grandmother would say. Your O.G. - Obtaining Greatness value is the future value of what you will release discounted by your character and integrity. You might "look" good, but your numbers might not add to greatness. Sometimes it's difficult to put others before yourself especially if you've been taken advantage of before. Understand, lack of trust will slow you down. You don't have to trust everybody but be sure there is a valid reason not to believe them before you make assumptions.

Subtract doubt

There's a saying that goes, "When in doubt, don't." If this is your motto and you are a person who doubts all the time; when there's an opportunity to be had, you won't. You won't be able to recognize it because your guard will be up and you don't want to get hurt. I understand. I don't want to get hurt either. One thing I learned on this journey is the more you protect yourself beyond what's healthy, the more you are isolated and separated from your greatness.

O.G. - Obtaining Greatness means you will take some risks in life. Most of us take risks all the time but become super cautious when it comes to our feelings and emotions. The old mindset said you need ice water running through your veins. It said you must be detached emotionally. A real O.G. feels. You can deny your feelings and ignore what you go through, or you can grow through it. Pain can be a guide to understand where you are and the changes needed to get you where you want to go.

Baggage Claim

Without the Release Law operating in our lives, we tend to hold on to what we should let go. Have you ever gone on a trip and tried to pack for all occasions and weather variations? That luggage begins to get heavy after a while and you leave no room for added happiness on your return trip. What about those bags filled with stuff that doesn't fit anymore? You can't put anything new in the closet because of all the old stuff in there. Life can be the same way. Relationships can become heavy after a while if the luggage isn't light. There's no room for my imperfections if you have your old boyfriend's shortcomings tucked away in a bag somewhere. If this issue isn't resolved the Release Law isn't operating in your life. The mess we allow ourselves to hold on to can cause great harm.

Hoarders

When the bags, luggage, and boxes of situations, events, and negativity get in the way of you living a normal life, you become defensive. It's not you that has a problem but everyone else. I have been there. As a child, I watched our home filled to the ceiling with stuff my grandma thought too valuable to throw out. As a man, I filled myself with emotional garbage that threatened to stink up my life. I didn't want to release it. But this is a heavy burden to carry, and at this point, an intervention may be necessary. How do you know if you've started hoarding your baggage?

1. Can you think of someone in your life, past or present, who has done you wrong and you can't forgive them?

Unforgiveness has robbed more "good" people of living abundant lives than any other bag you might be carrying. We will talk about this in more detail but know that it's not something we can ignore and have greatness.

2. Do you recognize any generational issues in your life that your parents or even grandparents might have dealt with?

Just like there are generational blessings there are generational curses, too. This is an area we need to observe because most of the stuff will go unspoken. No one talks about it or wants to acknowledge it. Make sure you don't continue this cycle because it will affect your children and theirs.

3. What are some of the annoyances you see in other people?

When we can't get along with other people, it can very well be what we are seeing in them, reflects what's inside of us. Our impatience with the shortcomings and character flaws of those around us are only noticeable to the extent they resonate with us. If there's nothing inside that resonates, we could ignore the behavior, and it wouldn't bother us as much.

4. Do you have unexplained ailments in your body?

Spiritual, mental and emotional issues tend to manifest themselves in sickness and "dis-ease." Chronic pain without an apparent cause and lingering illnesses can wreak havoc on the body. If you have been afflicted for a relatively long period of time without treatment success you may want to check your "heart."

If you answered yes or can affirm these questions, you need the Law of Release to operate in your life. "Well that's obvious," you may say. But you need to know how to get to that place where you're no longer carrying this heavy load. It's simple, but it's not easy.

Forgiveness is mandatory - I Apologize

I believe in being held accountable. I think we should hold others accountable, as well. This means when I fall short or make mistakes, I make sure I own them quickly and never play the blame game. Sometimes I'm too strict on myself. "How could I be so stupid?" I would say on countless occasions. Sometimes there was nothing I could do but I felt, and still feel, as a man you take responsibility. From this life outlook, I found if you don't forgive yourself it can be hard to forgive others. So, own your mess and get over it. All of it! There are some consequences. You have to deal with them. Take your time and manage those consequences the best you can. You can take responsibility for your actions right away. You want this to become second nature.

Now, that you have forgiven yourself, let us move on to forgiving others. This can prove more difficult depending on the pain inflicted and the amount of time that has passed since the incident. We are in the last chapter of Part I, focusing on "You." Forgiveness is for you. Sometimes it seems like we're letting the perpetrator off the hook and our internal longing for justice won't allow that. Sometimes we can attempt to force justice into our timetable and we're right back at chapter one. We will continue "holding" until we let go. That is the Release Law.

The more you are willing to detach yourself from, the higher you can go. You can hold on and be good (not really), but you must let go to be great. I like how talk show host and King of Comedy comedian Steve Harvey puts it, "You have to Jump! You jump by faith and allow God to take care of you and open your parachute at the appropriate time."

Forgiveness is the same way. The perpetrator may take years to change. Do you have that much time to wait? Put that in God's hands and take the first step to release you from the hurt. Will it go away overnight? It's possible but it probably won't. O.G. - Obtaining Greatness moves you forward acknowledging that there are things outside of your control and quickly fixes what you can. Here are five steps I use when I need to forgive someone or ask for their forgiveness.

1. **Pray** - This is always a good idea. If you are confronting someone that may be antagonistic and not open to the idea of reconciling, you need help from a higher power. Praying will prepare and keep you focused during this time.

2. **Confront -** This should be done in a way that diffuses the situation. The difficulty lies in controlling our emotions when someone else doesn't necessarily have the same intent. In this case, it will take some humility. State the facts and how it made you feel. Acknowledge your part played in the situation and apologize.

3. **Don't blame -** If the other party is not as open as you are don't place blame or point fingers. Forgiveness is for you more than it is the other person. The sooner you can detach the emotion from the behavior that hurt you, the sooner this is put behind you.

4. **Refocus -** Ask yourself, "How do I improve in this area?" How do you keep this from happening again? Focus on what is in your control and not on what happened. Don't become bitter or allow anger to set in then justify it as your way to cope, or not let it happen again. Focus on being a better you, specifically in the area the problem occurred.

5. **Release -** Forgetting can be hard, but you don't have to be controlled by what happened. The Release Law allows you to reap far greater returns than if you continue to hold on. Change your mindset if you think you will come up short or you're letting someone off the hook. Someone is being let off the hook, you!

This is the greatest gift you can give or receive, but it takes opening and allowing yourself to be a little vulnerable. Being vulnerable is something we struggle with even when we haven't been hurt. You may be wondering, "How does being vulnerable allow us to grow?"

You must trust the process - Vulnerability

When we talk about trust we are talking about being vulnerable. You can't have one without the other. When you were in high school and, you met a girl or guy that you really liked, you didn't show your true feelings until you had an idea the feelings were mutual. Why do we go through this charade? We don't want to be vulnerable. To be an effective leader or team player there should be a degree of vulnerability. When we permit ourselves to be exposed we show our real strength. If you do not allow yourself to ever be vulnerable, you cut yourself off from all the opportunities that authentic relationship brings.

Have you ever seen a movie where the guy attempts to serenade a young lady with no regard for rejection or embarrassment? How awesome is it to have the courage to go all in with no fear for what we want? If you don't allow a degree of vulnerability you will lack this freedom and a certain level of courage. Without this level of courage, you will never get the girl, or the guy or whatever your goal is. What would happen if we were to change our mindset from thinking it wasn't cool to show our emotions? We had to be a tough guy or be cool in everything we did. Never let them see you sweat, right?

Super Fly

Many times, in relationships, we end up with the same type of partners. Meaning that girl who always dates losers still dates losers. Likewise, the guy who frequently finds himself struggling to find Mrs. Right continues to end up with a whole lot of Mrs. Wrongs.

We used to have a saying about turning certain types of women into housewives. The same is said for men. To find that man or woman who will meet our needs in a relationship, vulnerability is a good trait to look for. I know, being open goes against everything you said to do in the past. But, if you want to find someone who would make a good parent rather than someone who's a good player or pole dancer, you'll change what you're looking for and where you look.

I had a fly make its way into my house from the outside and, in its attempts to find the outside world again, it kept repeatedly running into the bay window. The window was sparkling clean and a thousand times larger than the tiny house fly. No matter how hard the fly tried to reach its goal of escaping the confines of my home, flying into the bay window at increased rates of speed proved futile.

Have you ever thought that changing your approach didn't make sense because what you wanted seemed to be right in front of you? A change in perspective makes you acknowledge the "bay window" and turn to find the open door in the room. The right guy or girl in front of you will only be accessible if you decide to try another way and risk going against your old mindset. Release the former to experience the new. I guarantee you will yield more than the seed you sacrificed to plant.

Sowing machines

Some of my favorite memories as a child were the times I would spend with my grandma. When I came into the world on August 5, 1973, my mother was only 14 years old. Mom did the best she could do with what she had. My grandma poured into me my entire childhood. She gave me the love my mother was not mature enough to offer at that time.

One of grandma's favorite pastimes was sewing. My grandma made quilts, and this process always fascinated me. The way she'd take pieces of random fabric she found, or that was given to her, and made it into something precious was fascinating. What really amazed me was how she would take this valuable quilt and give it to someone who needed it. Grandma was a sower and the Release Law has kept her offspring for many years. It followed her 89 years and sustains me even today.

We all have something to sow. You have something that may not seem of importance to you but will bless someone else. All the people that donated those old clothes, blankets, drapes or other material to my grandma didn't have a need or see any benefit. With the skill of my grandma, more value was added by her quilting process. Grandma took an even higher value, the finished product, and sowed into the lives of other families. Let me also add that sewing, or sowing, keeps those holes out of your pocket (financially). This is powerful because these laws must become a way of life to develop them into our culture. We'll talk more about O.G. Obtaining Greatness culture in Part III.

Talk this way, walk this way

I've taught my children since they could speak to never allow anything to come out of your mouth you don't want to happen. In other words, stay positive. You must speak what you want to manifest. Operating under the Release Law can be as simple as offering a kind word or a smile to someone when you don't feel like it.

When we believe we have nothing to offer, we are not in an appreciative state. The right mindset says we all have something to give. The more our speech is in line with our vision, mission, and our goals, the easier it is for you to get your actions to align. The dissonance in our lives when what we say doesn't line up with what we do is not acceptable for an O.G. - Obtaining Greatness lifestyle.

You should say some things out loud so that you can hear with your physical ear, then your physiology meets up with your spirituality and psychology. This is the inner man and outer man working simultaneously together to achieve the desired state. By no means allow this as an excuse to say one thing while doing another. We're talking greatness here and the thought of gaming the system shouldn't even cross your mind. The only person you'd be fooling is yourself. If this is you, give this book to someone more deserving.

Start each day looking for ways to be a blessing to someone. Ask, "How can I add value?" This is the Release Law in action. You let go of any negative attitude, situation or person who can hold you back. At the same time, you pour positivity, blessings and add value to others. I have to continue reminding myself what's needed for this to work. O.G. - Obtaining Greatness is not the "O.G." you may be used to but, trust me, this works. The repercussions of this law are generational.

Understand that it starts with you. You are the only one that can improve your situation. Together, we change our individual circumstances and teach our children and grandchildren to perpetuate these teachings.

Exponential blessings

The Law of Release gives you the ability to take a little and make a lot. It takes much energy to operate in this law because it's opposite to how most of us think. The purpose of this book is to change the way you think. To change the way your team or your family thinks and to change the way that our culture thinks. Change your mindset change your life means just that.

There are many social-economic challenges and inequalities built into the system that will not change anytime soon. You can adjust your position right now. If you feel powerless, understand that the powerful will never relinquish what's theirs, without a fight. Don't relinquish yours! This is not a call to arms, but this is a call to realize if you will achieve anything significant or have abundant blessings, it's up to you. Don't confuse this with the scarcity mentality that says there is only so much to go around.

To achieve greatness on any level, you must be abundantly minded. As Billie Holiday would say, "Mama may have, papa may have, but God bless the child who has his own." Although this may not be gospel truth, there is much wisdom in that statement. What about God's children who don't have anything? I stand to tell you we all have something.

Abundance starts with using what you have in your hand regardless of how small that may be. When it comes to small things, factoring in God, less becomes more. An O.G. does things differently, but you must be careful because there are a lot of fake ones out there who insist on doing things the old way. If you want to keep on getting what you have been getting, then continue to do what you have always done. Change your mindset, change your life.

O.G. Code - Let It Go!

- Let go of all resentment. Focus that energy on something more productive.
- Let go of bad habits and any advice that stops you from thinking clearly.
- Let go of your past. This will weaken emotional ties that may cause you to backslide.
- Letting go of pride. This allows you to walk in forgiveness and keeps you level headed during dangerous situations.
- Let go of other's expectations. These are typically linked to your past and to an older version of yourself that's not who you are today.
- Sow into someone who can't pay you back, someone that you do not have a vested interest in. Any "good" person takes care

of those they love, the "great" go a step further.

- Sow into those that are wealthier than you. You adding value is not dependent upon the circumstance you find yourself in. Add value wherever you go.
- Sow positive energy into the atmosphere. Always be mindful of your mental state.
- Sow into your vision. Be sure to set aside an amount of time weekly to review and every day take decisive action toward your goals and what you want to accomplish in life.
- Sow into yourself spiritually and emotionally. Take care of your body; take care of your health. There is just one you and everything starts with you.

Conclusion - Lost Luggage

From understanding our holding patterns, until now, I hope you have let go of some weight that has slowed your process. Don't go back looking for it! This is tempting to do but understand, all the important stuff, you have with you right now. It has been said that some things are in life for a reason and some things are for a season. Don't sweat the small stuff. Stuff can and will be replaced with even better.

People, on the other hand, need to be handled effectively. Don't treat people like you manage things. I'm not saying there won't be people left behind in this process because there will. What we want to do is understand that God works through people. Before you could become successful in managing people, you learned to effectively manage yourself. You now have the tools to stand independently as a person ready to lead those you have influence over. Independence is just a first step. How do you multiply your efforts? This will lead us into Part II of our journey where we focus on "Your Crew."

Part II - Mission

For the Family

After God, the family is the center of importance.

Sacrifice your personal desires for your family.

Take care of your elders, take care of your children.

Be a father to others.

Chapter VI - Amateur Advisors
The Tradition Law
Be selective from whom you receive advice

The traditions of your tribe should be examined periodically for quality. Do they currently serve you and those you are responsible for?

We are family!

You were born into a family and, good or bad, you didn't get a say in choosing who you ended up with. This has been a fact throughout history. It is a blessing for some and a curse for others. The blessings passed from generation to generation have a significant effect on your actions today. The same can be said for anything negative.

Family can be like a business. You want each year, or generation, to be better than the previous. It's a "going concern." Meaning there is no end date. Over the years a certain culture develops within families, intentionally or by default. Your job is to acknowledge where you are and where you want to go. O.G. - Obtaining Greatness causes your vision to be larger than what you could ever do alone. It's your job to sort the tools and labor or, should I say, skillsets and people that will help you reach your destination.

We will continue the groundwork laid in Part I and look at our role in a new perspective, one conducive to running a great crew. Notice I didn't say good. The Tradition Law is a continuation from the Release Law. It gives you guidance on learned principles that have guided your life and the people you learned those principles from. Some of this is good stuff that will serve you all your life. Some of the people will grow with you and become great. But this law also deals with change. Change is difficult for most of us and, as an O.G., you must embrace it. An O.G. who does not like change might want to spend a little more time in part one of this book. It's all on you!

Family means different things to different people and there are many ways to define it. Let's start by looking at it from the traditional sense. This is where your first lessons are learned and where you meet your primary teachers. This is the starting point for what you learn and everything you will have to unlearn.

Russell Sprouts

Growing up in a single parent home was not uncommon when I was a child. My grandma was the head of our household and we didn't have much money. She was my great-grandma, the mother of my maternal grandfather. I knew her as "grandma." My mother's mom, my actual maternal grandmother, died before I was born. What we lacked financially, we made up in love. My grandma, or Mama Clara as she was affectionately known, would always brighten my day and I was her pride and joy as well. From sewing quilts, to working in her garden, to watching my grandma make canned preserves, I learned the value of hard work at an early age. She was my teacher before I knew I was being taught. I loved her dearly and still hold fond memories of sitting with her watching the Lawrence Welk show or Hee-Haw, two of her favorites. I think this is where my varied interest in music started. My granddad, Mama Clara's son, lived on my block along with other aunts and cousins. Russell Street was the campus where we learned our early lessons in life.

111

During my first ten years, Grandma was a significant part of my daily life. After, she moved into a senior apartment, leaving my mom and me in the home we rented. She suffered from a stroke shortly after that and my life was never the same. Grandma was my first teacher and I still hold those lessons to this day. This laid the groundwork for a very curious life. Who was your first teacher? Do you remember any of the early lessons you learned in life? I believe these early lessons set me up for greatness. Many of us can look at our grandparents and say that grandma or grandad was a real O.G. They had the O.G. -Obtaining Greatness mindset.

I can't say that my neighborhood was the best place to grow up, but it was a neighborhood full of love. Everyone looked out for and respected one another. We were and still are family. This affinity can have a way of locking you into everything the neighborhood had to offer, good and bad.

My neighborhood was in a typical blue-collar American city. This was during the decline in the automobile industry. Almost all my friend's parents worked for the automobile industry. This "industrial" mindset permeated the thinking of that time and everyone's goal was to "get in the plant" for a perceived steady job with good benefits. The eighties crack cocaine epidemic provided an alternative to back-breaking labor. You know the story, it plays out the same way across America. This was my campus and thus my "education" was limited to the levels of what I was immersed in.

John Maxwell in his book, "The 21 Irrefutable Laws of Leadership," talks about the "Lid" principle. It states that followers will not grow beyond the level of their leaders. If there is an exception, this individual will probably go on to lead. You can't take people to a place you have not gone. There is a talent drain on our inner cities that perpetuate this situation.

One of my early mentors in life worked in banking, but his office was eventually moved out of my neighborhood and relocated to another "market." Growing up, these wonderful people in my (and possibly your) neighborhood were well-intentioned. They poured into us to the best of their ability and many times this is not enough for greatness. We'll be good, but not great. The Tradition Law tells us to take everything good in our upbringing and early development and to discard anything negative. Continue to do this at different stages in life. Trimming that bottom 10-20% allows you to grow your potential and increase your capacity.

This is a process that will become a part of your growth. As you evolve from good to great, you will need more effective instruction and teaching. Ask yourself, "Will this degree provide me the knowledge I need to secure employment?" If you are looking to start your own business, maybe you don't need a degree. This is really thinking outside of the box and forward-looking versus how we've always done it. Perhaps you only need a certification. Some certifications require college degrees but an O.G. - Obtaining Greatness education is not the same as traditional education. Trade school, entrepreneurship, and online learning can possibly be more beneficial to the environment we live in today. "3251 Russell Street University" is not around anymore. I changed my mindset, and it changed my life!

In the beginning, God created...

Traditionally, the more you were perceived to consume, the more prosperous you were. This means if you have a new car, the latest gadgets or a fresh wardrobe you must be doing something right. Multiply this kind of thinking within a community and "Keeping up with the Jones" provides a false narrative of what it means to be wealthy. Or, what it means to be rich, hood rich. The vast wealth discrepancy can be directly linked to the mindset of producers and consumers. Yes, oppression and injustice and a litany of other problems plague our communities. These generational issues will take more time to solve. Time you don't have!

Producer and consumer decisions affect our pockets right now and this change in mindset will divinely place us where we need to be. Consumer-minded people have stuff. Producers have what I call "capacity." What is capacity? It's your choice level. The larger the capacity the higher our level of choices or options.

I remember when cars were sold without air-conditioning or power windows. These were, at that time, considered luxury options. Features that were optional years ago have become standard today. Capacity works the same way. Your decision to produce will dictate your lifestyle. As you expand your capacity what mattered to you before is not even a conscious choice anymore. It just is, and your options are now on a different level. Likewise, a consumer will continue being spoon fed whatever the "producers" can profit from (places like Madison Avenue and the term designed obsolescence come to mind). When you have the means of production, you can produce at the abundance level. This is a level where every need is met. Your entire thought process is now on how can I be a blessing to others. You live in the land of "more than enough." What happens when this is the thought process of your crew, family, or community? You solve your own problems. Before you say anything, think mindset. You must change your mindset.

There are three ways to create. One way is to take old ideas and refurbish them. In this fast-paced world we live in, the nostalgic longing for an easy way of life leaves many people searching for the historical and antique more than the brand new and contemporary. Getting off the grid, or at least away from our cell phones for a while, is a remedy to satisfy many needs. To be able to drive a car that's not somehow "tracked" or not have your picture taken at every turn is very appealing to some. Organic food is nothing more than food made the old fashion way (no pesticides).

The second way is to take old ideas and blend them with new ideas. This is where the bulk of "new" products come from with every new concept being a variation of something old. The razor has been in existence for thousands of years. The last hundred years the safety razor has given us a new product almost every year. Ideas will come to you in a flash of inspiration. Something new and innovative is just a daydream away. It's hard to think this way if you are not used to using your creative muscles. Traditionally, you don't grow these muscles. Most of the time we use our creative muscle for our employer and reap marginal benefits ourselves. We will challenge and change this mindset.

Lastly, you can innovate. Tradition can force you into a hard mold, but you must learn to use your imagination again. Innovation and ingenuity come to those who challenge how we've always done it and seek new, fresh, sometimes exotic ideas. How do you unlearn falling in line? Or, when do we see "go to college and get a good job" as a relic from our past that doesn't fit everyone anymore? This is the Tradition Law, challenging old ideas that don't propel us forward anymore. The only constant is "change."

Creative destruction allows you to create something new but not without destroying the old. In this case, mindset. We will go deeper into this topic of creation in chapter ten. Don't be surprised when attempted change is met with massive resistance.

Family Feuds

I'm going to do it. Monday morning I'm going into my managers' office and hand in my resignation. Ten plus years of my life, when is enough, enough? I must take my destiny back into my own hands. My wife was not too pleased and I was all too familiar with the phrase "happy wife, happy life." My mother didn't really understand either. Although she supported me in everything I've ever attempted, she never let the dissatisfaction of life propel her to do something different. I had other family members answer, "What college are your children attending? You have three college age, right?" Just when I was right at the edge ready to jump, I reneged. I listened to the sound of tradition and kept my "safe" paycheck paying job. I had temporarily lost the fight. Your family will almost never understand when you want to do something different. Especially if there is the possibility of discomfort.

Years ago, there was something called a caste system. This system would dictate a person's lot in life. If you were born poor you would probably expire poor. If you were born into wealth you might die a wealthy man or woman. Although this is not the way it is today, our tradition will try and creep in to make it so. It takes massive amounts of communication between the right people to break this system. Evaluate your life to see if these elements are present.

P.o.d.-cast

Do you pray over decisions? Don't! It sounds virtuous enough but there is a nuance that gets overlooked. You've already made the decision. Now, you want God to cosign on your plan. Pray for direction, use your mastermind and other trusted advisors for insight. Don't p.o.d.cast.

Typecast

Sometimes we get locked into a vocation or role based on who our mother or father is. If you come from this family this is what you do. You are an individual and to be typecast into a role not designed for you can bring a life of misery and not being fulfilled. You are just fine if you march to the beat of your own drum. Don't typecast.

Broadcast

Do you feel the need to tell everybody what's going on in your life? When you broadcast, you go beyond your four walls and the signal is picked up with anyone with itching ears to receive it. Some people are tuned into your frequency not to help, but to discourage and sabotage your plans. They will do this by sowing words of doubt and discord. If social media is your thing, tell what you've done, not what you plan to do. Just do it! Don't broadcast.

Forecast

The only people who need to know the forecast for what's about to happen in your household are the heads of that household and, to a lesser extent, the children depending upon their ages. Forecast in strict detail outlining probability and contingencies. This is not a one or two-day forecast, not even one or two weeks. This is an extended forecast. You can call it a climate chart. Sunshine, heat index, inches of precipitation. You name it, it's anticipated. Of course, you've done all your homework ahead of time and have monitored the seasons for a year or two. You know the patterns of the jet stream and the ocean currents. The key is to make your partner comfortable that you didn't just look outside, seeing the sun was shining and said, "The parade is this afternoon!" Give your partner every assurance possible and have a plan that can withstand you failing. Keep this in your household. Forecasts are on a need to know basis.

Simulcast

Every day and every hour monitor what's happening versus what was forecasted. Communicate this to your business partners, wife, banker, etc. with complete objectivity. Give worse case scenarios in your pro forma. This is hard sometimes because we like to paint the rosiest of pictures regardless of the reality staring us in the face. We can be optimistic, and have faith that our plan will work, but be fair to everyone and err on the side of caution. This will build the relationships as opposed to driving a wedge between them. What gets measured will get done. This is important when breaking out of what we've been rooted in. The temptation to return to the familiar can be overbearing.

Recast

You can change the weather. When you change your mindset, you change your life. If at any time you feel the need to adjust the forecast, don't hesitate to do so. Meteorologist recast all the time. There is no shame in adjusting. There is no honor in continuing down the path of destruction because you failed to check the weather patterns.

It takes strong leadership to carry this out in your household or business. I don't mean just forcing everyone to comply either. It takes patience and timing. You want to be efficient with most things in your life but, when it comes to people, you must be effective. This is the only way you will influence them.

Leadership is Influence

In our patriarchal society, fathers lead their households. Men are strong providers and protectors. The Tradition Law challenges old ideas that stagnate your growth and holds you back. The law also holds true to the beliefs that add value and drives us forward in significant ways. Everything traditional is not wrong. We don't throw the baby out with the bathwater. When we decide we want to grow and expand, there is pruning that takes place. I don't believe there are bad families. There are families that have experienced poor leadership.

The same can be said for our communities. There are even more companies suffering from the same maladies. Great leadership comes at a premium today. We can look no further than our politics to realize this.

Leadership is not the traditional "title" that gives us the positional authority over our subordinates. It's not the corner office or named parking space. If you think that the leader doesn't need to work as hard as everyone else, you have fallen for another misconception of what leadership is. A great leader will work harder than anyone else. A great leader will empower and develop his people. If there's someone with the potential to exceed him, there is no threat. There is only sacrifice on the leader's part to get the job done and make sure anyone under his influence is developed to utilize their full capabilities. There are no bad teams, only teams with ineffective leadership.

When your company is not growing, or is losing market share, the leadership must hold themselves accountable for any lack of progress. This is not finger pointing but a way of modeling what you want the company culture to look like. Addressing problems from the top down will always move faster than from the bottom up.

Accountability is critical in everything we do. O.G. - Obtaining Greatness is a no excuses lifestyle and, I can't say this enough, requires a complete 180-degree turn from the culture of blame. Some of us toss the word "great" around too loosely. Greatness will cost you something. Far more than you ever had to pay for "good." I really need you to stretch when it comes to these family relationships. Some of them are no good for you, and others will have destinies that are linked to your fate.

When no one is at the leadership helm, your team, family or crew will stagnate and continue to drift off course susceptible to anything happening to them. To be great you must be intensely deliberate. Tradition can be too comfortable and can lull us to sleep in mediocrity. We can be too progressive and lose valuable nuggets that have guided us through generations. Be intentional when you pick and choose.

A Family Affair

There is nothing like family. The family is central to the O.G. - Obtaining Greatness lifestyle. If you lead a team, you should love your team like a family. Your team members can tell the difference and this will cause them to dig deeper, or not. Whenever you have an opportunity to show love to your family, do it. Likewise, whenever you have a chance to appreciate a team member show that appreciation. As a leader, it is crucial you communicate your vision to your team and that you get buy-in from each team member. Planning a family vacation where everyone's need is met can be challenging. When everyone can provide input, differences can be minimized, and the object of having fun together is made easier. But what happens when you have a family member or team member that does not have any intention of contributing to the unit? This may be easier to deal with in a work setting then if you have to deal with the situation within your family. You have less, sometimes no decision, in who your family will be. There is a higher expectation of making contributions on the job which is incentivized by a weekly paycheck.

All my children are teenagers now and, at our house, everyone works. This is inside the house via chores and outside by various employment. I am not saying that this runs smoothly from week to week. As a leader I set the standards. These standards are within reach of each family member and requires them to stretch a little bit. But teenagers are teenagers and, from time to time, there are occasional interruptions in the household workflow. Accountability is everything and along with that is consistency.

In a team setting boundaries may be tested by team members from whom we have not gained a complete buy-in. If you do not hold firm, stay consistent and keep everyone accountable, you will see this situation continuously go from bad to worse. The object is not to fire the team member or to kick the wayward child out of the house, but to develop them to where they are operating in their full potential. We want to achieve optimal flow within our teams. As a leader, to accomplish this flow, some behaviors and habits need to go.

1. Uncontrolled negative emotion

The old-school way of cursing someone out and giving them a piece of your mind so they comply with your wishes does not equate with greatness. I don't know about you, but personally, if you disrespect me, then little matters after that. I'm not taking any advice from you and I may become even more entrenched in my behavior. This mode of operating is a relic from days gone by. Managers on the plant floor got the job done by any means necessary. As an O.G., the mindset is, "There's always a better way."

2. Leading by position

As a leader you should be out front. Leadership has nothing to do with your title or position. To effectively lead a team you should give them something to model. The hope you have for your team cannot be above the expectation you have for yourself. Don't ask them to do something that you would not do first. Where you are on the organizational chart, for the most part, is irrelevant. I don't want to "read" that you are my leader, nor do I want you to tell me that you are my leader. Show me that you are my leader.

3. Blame

Accountability is a reoccurring theme whenever we discuss these O.G. laws and cannot be discounted. Blame, on the other hand, will undermine the leader's influence and rightly so. Remember, you want to give your team someone they can mirror. If your team reflected you how much would they increase in effectiveness? This is especially confusing to children you are attempting to hold accountable. It always amazes me the level of culpability we keep our children to compared to the level we hold ourselves to. "Do as I say, not as I do" won't inspire greatness.

4. Avoiding Conflict

Issues that arise within your family or team should be addressed immediately. If not, all your small problems will become more significant problems and your big problems will cause failure. There is no sweeping under the rug when it comes to leadership. Ignore issues at your own peril. You are risking your team's success. If you are a parent in this age of social media, you must be even more aware of the problems your child will face. Most of the time those problems will not reach your radar unless you actively engage and risk conflict. Take the cell phone to see what's on it. With privacy comes responsibility. More maturity can lead to more "space." This will undoubtedly cause conflict and anything you find that is inappropriate will create even more conflict. Embrace this conflict. You may be saving their lives.

Confronting conflict and achieving positive results within your organization may feel unreasonable. But, remember O.G. - Obtaining Greatness means winning the long game. The short-term sacrifices will yield huge dividends in the long run. Some of us come from an "if it's not broke, don't fix it" culture and there was a lot that went undiscussed in our families. Some of our elders were masterful with the family secrets only to allow those secrets to resurface in the lives of their children and grandchildren.

We have dismissed some element of the past generation's leadership style, but you must recognize the tremendous value to be gleaned from their experiences. If you have the opportunity to engage the elders in your family or organization don't miss it. They won't be here forever.

Precious Metals

Most of us invest in either stocks or bonds, but we forget about the alternatives asset class. By alternatives, I mean real estate, commodities, and precious metals. When we talk about precious metals the first one that comes to mind is gold. Some investors don't like gold. It doesn't give any income, you have to store it, and it is just not as exciting. I believe within our families, communities, and organizations, we have something just as precious as gold. It too gets overlook because of our lack of interest in what it has to offer. Our elders should never be overlooked or disregarded because of our contemporary way of thinking.

Many of you are just like me. You are the first one in your family to go to college and, hence, the first one to "make it." I will not receive a monetary inheritance from the previous generation. They don't even understand O.G. -Obtaining Greatness lifestyle. They will read this book and be happy I am now a published author. The principles and the laws may be beyond their grasp. This, by no means, diminishes their value to us. Precious metals provide stability in inflationary times. If your ego gets so inflated that you can't remember where you come from, look at Grandma. Look at Granddad. Look at Big Mama and Big Dad, and Aunt Ethel, and Uncle James. It does not matter how far past "good" you have gone. It does not matter how much "greatness" you have obtained. If there were no "them," there would be no "you."

Anyone that is genuinely about this O.G. life always, and I do mean always, pays homage to those who have gone before them. This is very important because we have become a society that does not value our elders as we should. I fear that our young people, as impatient as they can be, will miss out on the value gained from the greatest generation that has ever lived.

Working in wealth management, one thing that really makes my blood boil is eldercare abuse. To think that after years and years of adding value, your last years are met with someone trying to take away your dignity. To age is enough but to be taken advantage of when you are most vulnerable is not right. These are our diamonds. They have been forged year after year after year. If we don't recognize the dazzling sparkle, and shine as well as the fortitude and endurance they provide our lives, then shame on us. I have said it before. They are the real O.G.'s.

This entire book is dedicated to regaining the character, dignity, and ethics that made them who they are. To sit at their feet and glean from someone who has gone before you, is an honor. You need them on your team. Here are some ways to give praise to those who have laid the foundation.

1. Seek opportunities to volunteer serving and assisting the elderly in care facilities.

2. Research your family history through your older family members who may still be alive.

3. Ask for advice.

4. Celebrate your elders on any occasion.

5. Seek the mentorship of an elder co-worker.

6. Recognize your impatience.

7. Acknowledge any elder in your presence.

8. Actively and intentionally show respect.

There is a spiritual aspect to honoring our elders. This is one of those intangible benefits that cannot be quantified, but it makes a huge difference in your life. The Tradition Law teaches us what to throw out of our lives, old mindsets, and what to keep and cherish. We are nowhere near great if we do not honor our elders. They are the rock, the strength, and pillars that uphold everything we do. The long game recognizes that they are who we hope to become.

O.G. Code - All in the Family

In your quest to an O.G. - Obtaining Greatness lifestyle, you can't forget that family comes first. The family is the basic unit of society. Your leadership skills will be sharpened by the way you resolve your family issues.

- Family comes first, but be selective in whose advice you follow. The level of thinking that got us into our problems is not sufficient, and we will need a higher level of thinking to get us out of our problems.

- Understand the role you play within your extended family. Be the change you want to see in others.
- Communicate your plan to your family and teach the O.G.- Obtaining Greatness principles to your children at an early age.
- Lead your team from the front. Don't ask anyone to do anything that you are not first willing to do yourself. You will work harder than any other member.
- Have a clear plan and objectives for your team. Don't expect them to operate effectively with vague instructions on where you are leading them. Remind them of the vision and mission often.
- Encourage your team and give them praise. Let elders know they are valuable and they are appreciated. Learn what their individual needs are and meet those needs.
- Empower your team to make decisions. Give them the ability, tools, and resources to get the job done. Lead them by example, but do not micromanage them.
- Always show respect. Never allow a negative situation to cause you to lose control and act in a way you will regret later.

Conclusion - Before I let go

When I was a kid, there was a song titled "Let's Get It On" sung by the late R&B artist Marvin Gaye. Believe it or not, this was my favorite song. Not because I understood what the song meant. I could have well been conceived to the song, as it was recorded in 1973. I loved this song because I heard my uncle playing it all the time. I remember Marvin Gaye was killed by his father when I was only 10 years old. These memories are of the fabric of my childhood.

I remember them so precisely because of the music that played a prominent role in our household. I'll admit, I didn't turn into a silky soul singer, but my music appreciation has helped me keep my head straight and foster my creativity. Before you choose to "Let It Go," remember The Tradition Law.

The Tradition Law helps us to develop skills and build teams that provide professional guidance based on where we want to go utilizing the strengths of where we've been. You develop your crew by sacrificing for your crew. The next chapter will show us how to enhance this by gathering help where we have deficiencies. The Collaboration Law is where we don't settle for anything but the best; the best from ourselves and from those we place around us.

When you're a successful business person, you are only as good as your team. You can't do every deal alone.

— *Magic Johnson*

Chapter VII - MBA Draft
The Collaboration Law
We are better together

Choose your behind the scene players carefully and build a reliable supply chain. Greatness is a team sport.

Help!

What do you do when you meet a problem you can't handle? When your abilities fall short and you can't tackle the task at hand, who do you call for help? You can handle most challenges that come your way. You can't control everything that comes your way and, if you are able to, you are playing in a league that's too small. Men, traditionally, have lacked in this area of accepting help and admitting their weaknesses. Although I think men struggle more with this, it is not limited to men. Ladies, how many times have you worn the mask of "I have it all together," when inside you were about to fall apart? Our level of maturity and personal growth will dictate the size of the challenges we attempt to face and our ability to ask for help with those challenges.

The Collaboration Law causes you to seek assistance where you normally would compete. Competition only goes so far and, while being easily undefeated can be good, it won't make you great. A sure sign you are aiming too small is when you are effortlessly knocking everything out of the park all by yourself, and there is no challenge. I want you to think big, but I want you to get the help you need to bring those big thoughts to fruition.

Focus on building out and preparing your gifts and talents to be integrated with a bigger picture. When you paint a picture of your ideal life, and all you have to offer, does that picture only include you? Do you attribute your success to you and you alone?

Unfortunately, however successful we may become, that attitude stops us from fulfilling our potential. Les Brown once told a story. He said the wealthiest place in the world was not the diamond mines or any other untapped precious metal or natural resource. It's not the intellectual property or the patents in the U.S. patent office. It's not even the cash reserve held around the world in different countries central banks. No, this place is where dreams go unfulfilled. This is the place where what you could have been, is laid to rest. You may have guessed by now where that place is and many of us will die with our dreams unfulfilled. If we could only go to the cemetery and dig up some of those dreams.

Another instance of wasted potential occurs when we attempt to do everything by ourselves. When you're the star on the team, it might feel like it is up to you to get the job done. That may be true, but it is also your job to get everyone else involved. Ask a leader and he or she will tell you that we are here to serve. If there is no one to help, it can take away from your leadership ability. Instead of building and bridging, you will end up tearing down and dividing. Again, focus on changing your mindset. There is much more to see and it may be just outside of your peripheral. As a leader, not only will you need to have good court vision, but recognize the game that is played off the court as well.

Front Office

You are a visionary, a player, a mogul. Your skill has been honed to a level that puts you in a class of your own. You see the big picture and can start out with a grand idea. You will fail without proper management. There is a misconception that the role of manager should be played by you also. It doesn't. This realization is critical in a competitive environment or a collaborative one. Who do you need to recruit?

As a sports enthusiast, basketball, in particular, I love to listen to the G.O.A.T. debates or who's the "greatest of all time." You will often have a player that takes the options of not attending college altogether and heads straight for the pros. Names like Kobe Bryant and LeBron James come to mind. Some would argue that the younger players are not mature enough to handle the stresses of playing in the NBA. Others say if a player has risen to the level of greatness to be drafted out of high school that, in and of itself, shows a level of great maturity. Is there a time limit on "greatness?" As an athlete, there is a limited window of opportunity to maximize your physical abilities thus having a successful career.

Sometimes our vision for what we will do off the court is just outside of our eyesight. If you get a solid ten years in the league, what do you do afterward? Ten years is a very long time relatively speaking. The level of success you have on the court will be in direct proportion to your teammates. The same is true when we consider the level of success you have off the court. When great players are drafted, they are momentarily put in the spotlight for that day. All the hard work and effort that led up to that day is not always showcased. Nor is all the behind the scenes deals, management and organization apparent.

You can't have a successful organization on the court without having success behind the scenes, off the court. In chapter eight you will learn about "The Family Business." It eventually has to operate without you. Plan for it.

The King James Version

I remember when I was a kid going over to my Uncle Jim's and

Aunt Ethel's house. One thing I remembered going into their home in the living room was the Holy Bible. This is something I know many of you can relate to. When I got my first home, I did the same thing. I had it right there on the fireplace mantle opened to Psalm 23. It has been said the Bible is the most significant book ever written and with the invention of the printing press also the most read reaching millions of readers all around the world.

LeBron James is arguably one of the greatest players in the league. He was one of those players drafted out of high school. It was 2003 and James was the number one pick for the Cleveland Cavaliers. Although he has had a storied career thus far, this book is still being written. Currently, at the age of 34, James may be able to surpass many more records and possibly claim the title G.O.A.T.

This is an example of on the court success. LeBron James is successful in many other areas of his life, but I want to focus on the Cleveland Cavaliers organization. I am quite sure a lot goes on that you and I as spectators do not get to see.

If you want to perform well on the world stage, you need a good front and back office. If you have had any level of success, make sure you thank your back office. Do you believe all your accomplishments were done by you and you alone? You don't have, nor think you need a back office? You could be right, BUT never an O.G. Whenever you see an athlete, actor, or anyone that does anything great they will have a long list of people they want to thank. They understand it's not about them and it is much bigger than they are.

In the case of the Cleveland Cavaliers, we loved LeBron James (currently with the Los Angeles Lakers). We celebrated him and, if you like the sport, you look forward to seeing him play for many more years. But if there is no NBA team management, there will not be any NBA team players. O.G. - Obtaining Greatness mindset is bigger than the Cleveland Cavaliers. What does the organization look like after LeBron? It's also bigger than LeBron James. What does his career look like with the Lakers? However you look at it, it's much larger than one man, or one team. This is The Collaboration Law.

The Book of Daniel

Dan Gilbert is an incredible businessman. From his real estate ventures in the city of Detroit to what he has done with the Cleveland Cavaliers organization, Gilbert's business acumen and eye for opportunity continue to grow his fortune. When he took over as majority owner of the Cleveland Cavaliers, Dan made changes that strengthened the organization. We never see the back office, but we know it's there. It's evident by what we see on the court. Your life is the same way. If I see you are successful and obtaining greatness, I know there is a back office that is making this all possible. Everyone knows their role. Unauthorized communication usually won't come from your "front office." Likewise, your bench players won't be recognized as stadium builders, but they play an important role. It won't work without them. Once again, stay with me. We're changing mindsets!

If the King James version is the brand, or what we have come to expect, at the O.G. - Obtaining Greatness level, we study the Book of Daniel, as it represents the prophecy of what's to come. These two ideas work together, but I don't want you to lose sight that you can be a person who cashes big checks and you can also be one who writes them. We're just doing it on different levels. Do you limit yourself because you have never done something before? Do you understand it's not how much money you make, but how much you grow and keep? If I asked you to grade the Cleveland Cavaliers basketball team's performance, as of this writing, you would probably give them a "D." I want to challenge your mindset and ask that you dig deep into the Book of Daniel instead of just having the King James version open on your coffee table. Instead of just watching LeBron play, study the man, study the organization, and the supporting cast. There are many other brands out there, but it's the content that will change your life. That content is the playbook, the instructions and those breakfast table conversations most of us never had. It's the relentless drive and dedication to your craft. Yes, there are O.G.'s in the NBA. I love hearing and seeing the business acumen of today's NBA players. From real estate to venture capital, I hope the day of the financially uninformed athlete is over. These are the type of "off court antics" I want our children to aspire to. I can't wait to see LeBron James, team owner! All of this happens through The Collaboration Law.

In the beginning was the Word...

When you think of God, you should consider Him as plural and as singular. Although, when you view yourself, most of the time it's from the perspective of just one person, limited by what you have to offer and no more. This causes you to have a limited view of yourself and your capabilities. When you began to view yourself in the image of God and see you how God sees you, then you get a glimpse of your real possibilities. Do you remember when you believed you could do or be anything? For many of us, we can't see that far back because it's been a long time since we held that kind of belief in ourselves. When you were a kid you may have wanted to be a doctor and a lawyer! The funny thing is no one could have convinced you otherwise. You were super confident and, even if you changed your mind the next day, you believed with the same bold assurance. What happened? As we transitioned through adolescence the expectations of others began to wear us down. The guidance counselors meant well, but judged students by their all "A" report cards, friends and, sometimes, parents. What was meant to be protection became obstacles to us believing in ourselves and becoming who we were called to be. Now, we need to unravel the layers of "security" to move freely in the direction we are called. Can we ever believe that confidently again? What do you need to walk fearlessly through this period of decay and destruction in your life? Is this what protection does?

The 'D' students

The first half of the twentieth century witnessed the birth of the automobile industry. A mass exodus from Southern states to Northern cities occurred allowing people the opportunity for a better life and a higher standard of living. No town flourished like the city of Detroit, Michigan. Detroit, in its heyday, had a population of over one million people. The big three automakers, General Motors, Ford, and Chrysler were all headquartered in Detroit, the home of Motown! It was called one of the greatest cities in America at that time. What happened? As the auto industry was lulled asleep by its own success and foreign car makers entered the market, Detroit's slow but deliberate downfall was exacerbated by the 2008 recession. This led to the largest municipal bankruptcy in U.S. history.

On top of that, mismanagement within local government tarnished the city's already downtrodden reputation. The description I just gave you is far from where Detroit is today. In just a few short years, we have seen this city begin to rebound, and it will soon be firing on all cylinders. Many people are moving back into the downtown area and are enjoying the urban lifestyle. From tech workers to startups to a robust service sector, the city of Detroit continues to grow its workforce. Detroit is home to four major league sports franchises all within the city limits as of 2017. The Lions, the Tigers, the Red Wings and the Pistons all call Detroit their home.

I share this story because there was a time in Detroit's history where the city was filled with innovation and ingenuity and believed it could accomplish anything and it fell into despair only to rise again. Today is your day to do the same. With a little help from the Collaboration Law, a D student can be just as, or even more, successful than all those straight A valedictorian types. You have good grades, ok but do you have grit? It's not important how many times you fall. Be sure you always get back up. The key is to get the right help and not fall prey to the status quo. Don't get boxed into thinking only one way. The old way O.G. (original gangster) cannot function in greatness. It's short-lived. O.G. - Obtaining Greatness involves getting rid of the past and embracing the new. Your mind may be set to the old way, but trust the process. Old habits will deliver old results. It will take faith to step into the unknown. It takes faith to be great. Surround yourself with great people you trust and take time to get the right chemistry.

The Speed of Trust

I love watching fast break basketball. With the right chemistry, it is like art when players are at their best. One key ingredient needed for a team operating at this high level is trust. Trust speeds things up and it allows us to do what we do best. Like intense listening there should be strong trust. Trust is built over time, and if you attempt to force it, you are doing more harm than good. Relationships take time to grow. To be effective you must accept that time. We want to be effective with people and efficient with things. When we attempt to be only useful instead of effective with people you run the risk of damaging the relationship. There are areas where trust is given without proof until you show me otherwise. Then there are instances where it should be established before we move one step further in our relationship. What are some ways we can gain trust in our relationships? Remember, it takes time to establish trust.

O.G. Code - Trust Bank

Personal accountability is part one of everyone's story. In other words, you must own it. This is extreme ownership because it is life or death, and you have a lot of people depending on you. Once you understand this, you will realize help is needed. The Collaboration Law allows you to do what you do best while at the same time trusting others to do what they do best.

- Every day do your very best and leave it all on the court. Win or lose, you have given it your all, and those around you will appreciate it.
- There will come a time when you will have to dig deep. When you think you have given your all, more will be required of you. Being able to deliver in clutch situations becomes a way of life.
- There will come a time where you will temporarily need to turn the reins over to someone else altogether. Your strong sense of faith and understanding that this too shall pass will allow you to make it through difficult times.
- Understand that God works through people. It's great to get

the job done yourself, but you can accomplish so much more when you understand this principle.

- Don't hook up with anyone whose values are contrary to your vision. These short-term gains will trip you up down the line and cause you to lose focus.

- Lead with a servant's heart. You must love people. This does not mean you won't have your moments of solitude, but to serve, you should be visible. People don't care what you know until they know how much you care.

- Take time to rejuvenate. You may experience times of extreme fatigue. When this happens, there must be a quiet place that you can go to refresh. Don't feel bad taking time out for you.

- Surround yourself with people who are smarter, stronger and faster than you are. You should never be the most intelligent person in the room.

- Understand that some people are only in your life for a season. There will inevitably be times when people depart your life who you thought would be there for the long haul. When this happens, send them off with your blessing.

- Understand that this is bigger than you. Give your team a sense that it is more significant than them as individuals also. This goes back to understanding your "Why," and making sure everyone else's "Why" has common ground.

Conclusion - In God We Trust

Before 1973 the United States currency, the U.S. Dollar, was backed by gold. We called this the gold standard and so many dollars purchased one ounce of gold. Our money has since become what we call fiat currency. This means it is backed by the full faith and confidence of the United States government. Although there was no physical backing, we believe the value is there. Barring any governmental collapse this system will hold true.

Walking by faith is a tough thing to do. Everyone has confidence until it is exercised. When you must use your faith you are releasing control. Trusting the people God has placed in your life, is an exercise and discipline you will need when it comes to putting it all on the line, without any physical evidence of your goal being realized. God works through people.

The Collaboration Law will help you recognize who's in your corner and who is likely to stay there. Some of them are people you pick and choose and some are inherited. They may not be your family, and they will come from unexpected places. We will also explore if we have everyone in the right positions on our squad to grab some wins. Successful people always have someone behind the scenes. No one achieves considerable success by themselves. Sometimes we grow up as loners. Many of us have grown up with trust issues and have learned to do everything on our own. That can make you good, but it won't make you great. Now, we will look at the family business where you don't join in, you are born in. You did not plant the seed, but you might reap a return from someone else's investment.

I got my start by giving myself a start.

— *Madame CJ Walker*

Chapter VIII - Family Business
The Investment Law
Entrepreneurship is a wealth creator

Manage your risk and expect an appropriate return. Prepare your successor and empower your people.

Understanding the Game

Many products have become commodities and what we are really purchasing are people and personalities. I believe everyone has the ability within them to hustle, and hustle is good. A business requires more organization and competence of how the system works. As far as those differences go, the internet is changing everything. To get a good understanding of these differences between a business and a hustle let's talk about the two starting with a hustle.

In this new economy, you will hear a lot of talk about having a side hustle. Sometimes this is money made "under the table," or money that's not reported to the government for tax purposes. If you are not careful, your side hustle could get you in trouble with the government. Three people you do not want to mess with is the I-R-S. I always advise seeking professional help if there are questions concerning your taxes. There are legal ways to pay less taxes. Over the years, I've become more sensitive in this area as my financial affairs become more complicated.

One thing that distinguishes a hustle from a business is most of the time, for a hustle, it's all about the money. If you obtain more enjoyment from your side hustle, then you do from your regular nine to five job, you may have it backward. Maybe your side hustle is what you should be doing full time. Lastly, your side hustle is all about you. It adds value to you and you alone.

Now, when we talk about business, there are a few things I want to point out. If you want a real business, and not a glorified job, your business should be able to stand all by itself without your assistance for a given period. That should be the goal at least. This means the business does not go out of business because you decided to take a vacation. A business may provide employment for others besides the owner. A business is measured with exacting detail compared to side hustles. This is because your entity is expected to go on indefinitely. You can end your side hustle tomorrow. A business, at the end of the day, increases value for the shareholders even if you're the only one. Many times there are other stakeholders, but you have an exit plan. This can be selling in five years, or passing it to your heirs. Your influence will begin to stretch and touch the various stakeholders which include your employees, the community you serve, your family and any other philanthropic beneficiaries. From an O.G.'s perspective, consuming less and producing more is enhanced when we travel this entrepreneurial path of becoming a business owner. When you think business, think exit plan. This is the difference between having additional income and building wealth.

This chapter has two parts. First, it's about the entrepreneur in each of us. If the game of entrepreneurship is not for you many, if not all, of the principles you will learn in this chapter can be applied to your nine to five (or seven-three, three-eleven, eleven-seven job). I would never encourage someone to quit their job without a solid plan and the preparation needed to be successful (Like one-two years of savings, no debt or at least a manageable amount and buy-in from your spouse). If entrepreneurship is for you, you should know you will work a lot harder and longer than you do nine to five.

I do believe many of us who work in corporate America are underutilized, or are unfulfilled in one way or another.

Second, we will reiterate that you are not in this alone. Remember trust? The only way you can widen your reach and improve your efficiency is to duplicate yourself. The previous two chapters gave us insight into how we build our crew. Now we want to put them to work. This O.G. - Obtaining Greatness mindset and lifestyle utilizes multiple streams of income. It balances the need for more "stuff" with the enjoyment of richer life experiences and more time. I call this The Investment Law.

Strictly Business

When I was in high school, l would watch anything with Halle Berry (no "Jungle Fever," but she had me at "Boomerang"). In the movie "Strictly Business," Halle Berry stars as "Natalie," a party promoter who wanted to start her own nightclub. One of my favorite movies is the Godfather. In this movie, Vito Corleone is in the olive oil business (wink, wink). Vito Corleone's son, Michael, seeks to legitimize his father's operations. He is college educated and feels no need to continue in a criminal enterprise. Michael, through his political and corporate connections, tries very hard to make this happen and it almost works out. My wife and I like to binge watch TV on the weekends. We came across the TV show "Power" starring rapper 50 Cent and Omari Hardwick. Hardwick plays a character that goes by the name "Ghost." Ghost is attempting to leave his criminal enterprise and everyone connected to it to go legit as a, you guessed it, nightclub owner. There is something to be said about the individual that risks it all on themselves for the American dream. There's a big debate over if modern-day corporate America equates to the American dream. For me, it's all about freedom and choice. Others will sacrifice this liberty for perceived stability and security. I never felt too secure betting on someone else, and only recently became strong enough to bet on myself. I had to ask myself if I wanted to be a consumer or a producer? "It's like Lotto, you have to be in it to win it," the song says. There are no Lotto-like odds when you bet on yourself but there is some risk. It is possible to pawn your way across the chessboard of life to become another piece that's more valuable, but why not start out as a king or queen in the first place? If you have a job, keep your job. You will know if and when you're ready. Preparation is key.

Learning the language

Can you imagine what it's like to be in a foreign country and not know how to speak the native language? Imagine meeting someone on the street. You are desperately trying to get to your destination, but you only know a few word phrases, none of which seem to evoke a navigational response from anyone else on the street. Many businesses are not translating, and most find this out eventually (50 percent fail in the first five years). For some reason accountants don't always rank high in the "MBA draft," though they should. Accounting is the language of business, and I've seen many small business owners who didn't know the difference between a debit and a credit or a P/L (income statement) and a balance sheet. Don't even start with cash flow. Then there's inventory, raw materials to make the product and labor. If you are the only labor, don't plan to stay that way. What's your exit strategy? Start with the basics, assets equal your liabilities plus owners' equity. Equity is what you, the owner(s), have left over after everyone that you owe has made a claim on the company's assets.

On the TV show, "Power" Ghost's best friend Tommy was always concerned about moving the "product." As soon as inventory would come in, you wanted to get it out as quickly as possible. As the "connect," Tommy sold product on credit or under a consignment agreement; a lot of it. On his balance sheet revenue looks very strong but that was not the whole story. Once the product left Tommy's hand it was considered revenue. Now, the issue is with collection. Many business owners find themselves in a crunch without proper credit management. In Tommy's situation, there are not a lot of doubtful accounts because the consequences are a lot more severe than for the average businessman who doesn't pay his bills. Beware of increasing inventories. Beware of growing credit sales or accounts receivables. These are the details that must be attended to in any business and if they aren't, see the 50 percent statistic above. You don't have to be a finance MBA to run your business, but it wouldn't be a bad investment to hire one. It's a lot easier to recruit and retain a loyal crew when the company financials are in order.

Integrity is good business

Under promise and over deliver. This is always my goal when doing business with someone. It doesn't matter how large or small the transaction, being able to keep your word reaps great dividends. When you have other people working with you or for you, you owe it to them, and to yourself, that your business is always in order. Sure, things happen, I understand that, but for others to buy into your vision, your integrity should be impeccable. It's not that you set out to purposely deceive anyone when you overextend yourself, but when you're not completely honest, that is precisely what you are doing. Fool me once shame on you, fool me twice shame on me. Eventually, you will find no one wants to work with you. You will be known for running a crew that can't be trusted or a bootleg business. You could even lose influence in your home. Your partner or your children would take everything you say with a grain of salt.

Sometimes overextending yourself is not worth this risk. You must set yourself up to win. I do not promise more than I will be able to deliver. You want to practice this not only with others but also yourself. There is no getting around this. As an O.G., one who's Obtaining Greatness, you must keep your word.

The smartest person in the room

The O.G. - Obtaining Greatness mindset tells you to stay surrounded by people you want to emulate. People who will stretch your mind and facilitate your growth; people who are experts in their field. In business, it is imperative to keep on top of your game. This includes your entire industry, not just your company. If this seems like an overwhelming task, you should appreciate surrounding yourself with people who have the answers you don't have. Too many times we are intimidated by people smarter or more prosperous than us. If you have a fragile ego this can hinder you from greatness. Have you ever witnessed the manager who is surrounded by yes men? No one dares to step up and tell him the truth either because he likes it that way, or because of a lack of courage. I read a book when I was a kid called "The Emperor's New Clothes." You may have heard of it. If you don't empower the people around you, you will end up looking foolish. Your crew cannot simply be a bunch of yes men that do whatever you say, not thinking for themselves. You are in business for yourself, but you are also in the empowerment business.

One of my goals in business is to make the people in my inner circle very successful. If one of my guys grow to the point where it is time for him to strike out on his own then he will have my blessing. I will give my opinion on their decision and try my hardest to make sure they are a success as they go forth. Now, you may think, what if this person becomes a competitor? Nothing I do comes from a place of fear. Whenever I have operated from this space in the past, I've found that it's a very barren place to be. What God has for you is for you and no one can change that. This is especially true when you are operating from a place of gratitude and abundance and have the other person's best interest. The smartest person in the room cannot be you, or you're in the wrong room! Become comfortable being uncomfortable. Embrace it and watch your confidence level skyrocket.

The O.G. - Obtaining Greatness mindset is not the loner mindset. Now, don't get me wrong, sometimes it is good to be alone. But notice I said, "good." Being alone was in Part I. If you want to make it all the way to greatness, you will need the help of others. Nobody does it all by themselves, and if they do, they haven't done very much. Have you ever been accused of being a know-it-all? Do you have a hard time accepting the opinion of others? Here are some ways you can tell if this is something you suffer from.

1. I always feel a need to correct others when they're wrong.

Sometimes it's not what you say, but how you say it. But understand, most of the time, it doesn't even matter. Being in listening mode isn't a bad thing. Especially if you don't have anything positive to add to the conversation. If you are right most of the time and other people are always wrong, check yourself. You're in the wrong circle or have a slightly twisted perspective.

2. When I'm wrong in conversation, I just let it go.

One word, integrity. You are slipping out of O.G. territory if this is you. You want to flee the very presence of evil. If you are not spiritual let me put it this way. The ethics I must adhere to in the banking industry holds me to what's called a fiduciary standard. This means every decision I make concerning you must be in your best interest, not mine. Don't allow the rule of the world to be higher than your personal standards.

3. I never ask questions.

Even if you know the answer, confirm it. If you are assuming on serious issues you could jeopardize not only you, but anyone relying on you. Don't let your crew down because you felt a certain type of way asking for clarity, even if you did know.

Here I Go Again (on my own)

Sometimes I don't make the effort to really get to know people in my life. I know I miss out on a lot of opportunities to grow and develop possible friendships. I mistakenly thought I didn't have the patience for other people's ignorance. The truth is I was impatiently ignorant. Some of my ignorance could have been cured by engaging people. People are your greatest asset. Never forget this. Most companies will agree, a few will even back it up with their actions.

I cannot stress this fact enough. O.G. - Obtaining Greatness is not something you accomplish alone. I heard leadership guru John Maxwell once say, "It's lonely at the top because you didn't take anyone with you." I would add that it's not even the top, but a plateau you've come to without the proper tools to keep climbing. Those tools are other people. Everyone is not a snake. You will need to trust someone.

If you think you're lonely now...

It is important to do what you are called to do while you have the strength and ability to do it. While your physical strength may wane over your later years, your mental capacity to lead should increase with time. In the days where you have both make the most of it. In the book of John 9:4 it says, "I must work the works of Him that sent me, while it is day: the night cometh, when no man can work." Have you ever regretted not acting on something? Fortunately, most <u>good</u> things can be recouped.

Procrastination can allow you to miss out on those great things. People in your life that you should have poured into and developed will eventually pass by and be developed by someone else. The time spent at the feet of your elders is a limited window of opportunity. So is the time of your children sitting at your feet and being nurtured. Opportunity has a way of leaving you cold and alone if it's neglected. We always realize the neglect in hindsight. Someone once said it's better to be prepared and not have an opportunity than to have an opportunity and not be prepared. It's never greener on the side of procrastination. Appreciate your people because "tonight" is coming.

Reflections of you

What gets on your last nerve? Is there something you just happen to notice in people that just sets you on edge? When I was younger, I had a hard time with arrogant people. I thought how can anyone be so full of themselves. This got on my last nerve, and it kept me from approaching people I possibly could have had excellent relationships with. I would see someone, and if they didn't speak to me, I didn't talk to them. They were annoying. They were prideful and envious. They were stuck on themselves and they were… they were me. You should be careful because the thing that annoys you the most about folks is usually the thing that is in you. If it wasn't in you, it wouldn't resonate as much.

If you don't attempt to pour anything into people, don't expect to get anything out other than your reflection. This is a part of the Investment Law. Nothing risked, nothing gained. You take a risk with the people you let into your life. Do you remember "The Speed of Trust?" If trust is built over time, it accelerates your returns. If there is no trust then you'll play it safe. This is a hard lesson to accept. Remember, O.G. - Obtaining Greatness, change your mindset and change your life. Stop thinking like a "good" person. Have you ever heard someone say, "I'm a good person so I can't be...?" You fill in the blank. You will get out what you are willing to put in, and if that's nothing, you'll see a reflection. How do you choose to see people? Are they your greatest asset? Do you see the greatness inside your brother or sister? That mother who spent all your childhood, and most of your adult years, to get her life together, do you see the importance in her? These are O.G. questions because you are not a blamer. You are not here to get what you can get or take what you can. You are a giver, you are Obtaining Greatness. Does this mean you allow yourself to be run over and disrespected? No, you are above this mess and can't be touched by it. If you're not quite there yet, stay with me. It is a deliberate effort to see the best in someone. There's some good in the worst of us and some bad in the best of us. Unfortunately, if you can't see anything significant in me, it will be tough to see anything significant in yourself. You will see a lot of "good" and it will lead you to believe it's "great," but it serves only you. If something is only self-serving, it does not belong on the plane of greatness. "But he that is greatest among you shall be your servant" (Matthew 23:11 KJV).

Serve, Lead, Empower

In today's leadership curriculum, you may hear the term servant leadership. If there are any areas in our lives currently that we enjoy success, there was probably a servant leader that came before us and empowered us to do what we do. What is the servant leader? Seven areas make up the servant leader:

1. The servant leader adds value.

Have you ever heard the expression everything you touch turns to gold? Well, this is also true of the servant leader. In every capacity the servant leader will add value wherever he or she involved. Not only is value added, but that value is effectively multiplied through teamwork.

2. The servant leader connects.

Before the servant leader requires you to labor in any way, there is a connection that is made. That connection is the emotional connection seeing you as an individual first and not just a means to an end. Servant leaders touch the heart of followers and are concerned for their well-being first.

3. The servant leader shares his vision.

He does it in a way that allows his followers to see, hear, and feel it. Followers then take the leader's vision on as their own, and this enables oneness of purpose. Servant leaders are effective in getting you to see what they see.

4. The servant leader goes first.

This is leadership by example, and before servant leaders ask anything of their followers, he or she has already demonstrated how-to, where-to, and what to do. This is important. A servant leader will work harder than his followers.

5. The servant leader has a process for getting things done.

If you lead people they must be confident in your ability to get things done. A proven method will facilitate this confidence, and thus enhance your leadership ability. This gives followers incentive to give you their all and they know where they fit in to do their job.

6. The servant leader sets limits.

These limits are just outside what's thought of as possible. This allows the team to stretch and tap into abilities they did not know they had. Develop a habit of winning.

7. The servant leader empowers their people.

To multiply your effectiveness, a leader must duplicate himself through his team and give them the authority to get the job done in their own unique way. This empowerment is also a confidence builder because the team member can take ownership over his assignment.

Serving and leading are synonymous when it comes to leadership. One comes with the other, and when people are involved, there is a certain degree of care that is used. Again, you want to be efficient with things, but effective with people.

A leader understands their people are the greatest asset and they will treat them as such. People are the vehicle that allows us to travel from point A to point B. If you have a vehicle and you believe that vehicle to be a prized possession, you will regularly change the oil and provide all maintenance. You will keep the vehicle clean. You will push it to its boundaries when you are on the open road. You proactively look for and attempt to sense anything that doesn't seem right with that vehicle.

Up with people

In this world of short-term profits and quarterly earnings, the refrain "people are our greatest asset," is often heard but seldom shown. In our efforts to drive efficiencies, we can unknowingly diminish the long-term returns. Think about it. Some companies are afraid to develop people to their fullest potential because they think it's bad for business. They may become competitors. But, what happens when you don't improve your people to their fullest potential? It hinders you and it frustrates them.

In Part I, we talked about the abundance mentality. O.G. - Obtaining Greatness mindset does not feel threatened by anyone on his team, his crew or family. In fact, a true O.G. will continue to reproduce himself. What happens when we have a population of people living the O.G. - Obtaining Greatness principles in every aspect of their life? We will have a community that is self-sufficient, a community that is able to defend itself, and a community with a culture of greatness. This is the type of community that allows each member to not only grow as individuals, but to fulfill their God-given destiny and leave a legacy for those who come behind them. If you can't lift people then you can't grow to O.G. status. If you are intimidated by those around you, you will probably end up being the smartest person in the room.

The family office

As a portfolio manager, I had friends in the business that managed assets for one family, or for a few individuals of one family. These were generational assets started by an elder family member who may have had a successful business. Families like the Ford's or the Walton's come to mind, but there are thousands more that you have never heard of. Again, an O.G. plays the long game, and this involves planning on a level most people fail to comprehend. What net worth does a family need to have their own family office? A place to start, about $10 million. Do you consider this amount impossible? Fly high O.G.! You will most likely start at a smaller amount but think, "Mindset!"

Now, of course, many of those who will benefit from the family office did not necessarily contribute to establishing what funded the office. This is the true nature of wealth. It is not necessarily for the person that generated it, because you can't take it with you. Your most important assets are time and people, and since each of us are limited in time to the number of years we live, people are our most important resource. Your family office is providing much more than the money management for your family. It's offering a way of life that stretches far beyond the initial person or persons who established the office. That way of life may come in the form of a college education, cultural experiences, new world perspectives, and the increased probability of growing to provide for the next one, two or even three generations.

Wealth is not always equated with dollars and cents. I like to measure it in years. A more exact measure will be in the number of lives you've touched. Based on the people whose lives you have made a difference in, will you need a "family office?" Or, since your deposits (lives you touched) aren't that great, will a simple passbook savings account do for you?

O.G. Code - Appreciated Assets

- Let your people see you hustle harder than they do. Always lead from the front, lead by example, and never ask anyone to do something that you would not do yourself.
- Remember, you are in this for the long game and be strategic in maximizing the number of lives you touch during your lifetime.
- Don't allow wisdom to escape your generation. Treat your seniors with the honor and respect they deserve. Even if you don't understand, credit that to your ignorance and not theirs.

- Understand not everyone will view things the way you do. This is okay, and if they're willing, they can contribute in ways you may have not thought of.
- Do not become the smartest person in the room. Surround yourself with people who are more intelligent, more creative and who can show you a different perspective.
- Know the strengths and talents you possess but more importantly the powers and abilities of those in your crew. Cultivate those gifts so they serve the greater good.
- Empower your people to lead. Help them to become the best version of themselves and do not be afraid of their success. Recognize where one has the potential to grow beyond what you can offer. There is no lack by allowing them to fly.
- Entrepreneurship is honorable and should be sought after as an alternative to corporate America. Fear stops most people. Sometimes we can be good and scared, but an O.G. will do it despite doubt and fear.
- Add value in every place you serve. You set the temperature, and when you show up on the scene, things should get better. The environment should be more joyful, the energy level should increase, and there should be clarity of purpose.
- Learn the language. Don't be afraid to expand your knowledge of the basic skills that will allow you to function in the business world. This is essential if you will have a good handle on your financial affairs.
- Calculate your return on investment. More specifically, measure everything you do. What is not measured probably will not get done.

Conclusion - Grandfather Clause

Born in rural Mississippi, Rowan Buckley was forced to travel to the "North" after an unfortunate accident with a white man in his hometown. He secured employment with an auto plant. Roy, as he was affectionately called, went on to father five children and had many more grandchildren, great and great great-grandchildren. He worked many years for General Motors retiring in the early 1970's.

Working in the auto industry was a step up from sharecropping, and I can imagine the manufacturing facilities of his day didn't compare in cleanliness, or safety to those of today. Roy paid the price to come here, and I believe his offspring are reaping the rewards of his decision. My children did not have the opportunity to meet their great-grandad. I have very few memories. But I do know the R.O.I., or return on investment, of his coming here can't be measured in dollars and cents alone. When Roy left Mississippi he was all in 100 percent no turning back. Fearing change can become a tax on your livelihood and your offspring's. My after-tax gross income is increased because I was exempt from that "Mississippi taxation." Roy's investment continues to pay dividends. An O.G. remembers where he comes from.

What happens when you're Obtaining Greatness and you connect with others who are on the same path? We have talked about organic growth which is the growth from within your business, family or organization. There is another type of growth that will cause you to stretch even more. External growth will push you even further outside of your comfort zone. If you're going to excel at anything, it must happen outside of your comfort zone. O.G. - Obtaining Greatness, takes you far outside of comfort into being fearless. You are fearless of what's different. Will you allow your differences to paralyze or propel you?

If you don't understand yourself, you don't understand anybody else.

– *Nikki Giovanni*

Chapter IX - Growth Stock
The Allocation Law
Increase your risk tolerance

You must take some risk to grow. Your focus has been on more income, now, it should be equity.

Too big to fail

The Allocation Law reinforces the fact, this is not about you. If The Collaboration Law, which we discussed in chapter seven, was about finding the right people, The Allocation Law is the 30,000-foot view that aligns different organizations, families, communities and institutions. If The Collaboration Law aligned the right people, The Allocation Law combines the right teams. You understand the team, but what about the league? You are limited as an individual. Honestly, your team may be limited in what they can accomplish without collaboration with other teams. When I quote the scripture Matthew 6:23, "I can do all things through Christ…" I must remind myself God works through people. When I quote the scripture Ephesians 3:20, "Now unto Him who is able to do exceeding, abundantly above all…" I must remain open to where this "above all" will come from, or should I say, through. Who will God use? Because, again God works through people. The recurring theme here shows us we can't do it alone, and if you feel God is on your side, you better love people. Allocation, in its most basic form, is bringing together different elements to achieve a goal. The whole can be greater than the sum of the parts. In wealth management, we collect assets from different asset classes to build a portfolio. You can allocate with different people or cultures. You can assign to different ideas and solutions to solve problems. Our creative juices begin to flow when we master this law. There is always a way and we must figure out the right combination. Let every treaty you enter into be mutually beneficial.

If you are a spiritual man or woman then you have everything you need to succeed. Now that's easy for me to say without knowing your individual circumstances. Sure, your faith is a game changer. It makes up for everything you lack, and blended with hard work allows you to be successful. If you are a man or woman of faith, how can you think any other way? We are more significant than our failures. I don't mean just in the natural sense, but also in the supernatural. I don't know many people who would serve a God they believe could fail them. We understand, by faith, if our life is not going according to the plan we laid out, we can adapt and prepare for an even greater blessing than we anticipated. You never know who you'll cross paths with. Keep the right mindset and you understand what you need can be one introduction or handshake away.

Have you ever had a good time then hooked up with someone else who was having a good time? Together you both had an even better time than you could've had alone. The Allocation Law allows us to scale. When I have an idea, I ask myself is this scalable? Or, how big can I grow this? The O.G. - Obtaining Greatness lifestyle is distinctive and there are values that won't be compromised.

Don't allow foreign entities to dilute the inherent power you possess. You must understand different people have different strengths and different weaknesses. Bridging your strengths, and compensating for any weaknesses will allow you to become even stronger in the long run. The Allocation Law enables you to take the vision from concept to design, and provides the insight necessary when operating in unfamiliar territory. This brings more clarity to the vision being bigger than you and even bigger than your team.

This is where we begin transforming from building individuals or families/organizations to building dynasties. You will need to "reach across the aisle," something you might not be used to. It takes time. This is multi-generational; just do your part.

Mergers and Acquisitions

"He that finds a wife, finds a good thing and obtains favor from the Lord (Proverbs 18:21)." When you read that scripture what comes to your mind? Marriage truly is a blessing and it's important to note that it can be vital in the difference between good and great. There's almost no limit to what two committed individuals can do when their actions are combined in a spirit of harmony. Scripture says, "One can put a thousand to flight and two can put 10,000 to flight." I like God's math! This is a prime example where the whole is greater than the sum of the parts. To move to this level of greatness, you better put in the work outlined in Part I, beforehand. If you didn't, and you're married, there's an excellent chance you are in a "marital holding pattern."

Ultimately, we want to leave a legacy for our family and community. That legacy, in no small degree, will consist of your gift and your contribution. One of the most challenging parts of the O.G. – Obtaining Greatness journey is introducing external forces that must be carefully vetted to prove worthy of our connection. This is not the connection that we pick up or put down hastily, but one that is carefully considered before embarking on our legacy mission. When we meet someone and start developing a romantic interest in them, we don't always think like an O.G., and sometimes not even with our "good" senses. This is an area of your life where you need to be very deliberate about who gets that close to you. Do you remember the smartest person in the room? What about those amateur advisers? Don't fish in polluted waters. It seems obvious but many times the environment we catch fish in has not been highly cultivated, and it is not conducive to our long-term goals and strategies. When it comes to the heart, we can make some foolish mistakes. Here are some ways that will allow you to fish in fresh water. You want to attract quality fish that, upon inspection, you can keep as a prize, or inspect and throw them back out for further development. Some of the fish you catch will not have grown to maturity yet.

When forming a partnership...

Get informed. Ask questions, and upon hearing the answers to these questions, pay attention to if this person is being transparent with you. Do they mind being vulnerable? Do they enjoy just talking about themselves? Do they ask you questions? Is this just a way to deflect from the problem or question you asked? You can tell quite a bit from these initial conversations, or lack thereof. Whether you ignore these clues or not will be the difference between good and great and even misfortune in your life.

Move deliberately. An O.G. feels profoundly but does not make decisions based on feelings alone. Know the difference between your gut instinct and your infatuation. Before you commit to anything be sure your research has been done. These types of decisions are not summed up in one-page essays, but often dissertation-level research.

Pay attention to details. Have you ever heard the saying, "the devil is in the details?" Sometimes we can do everything we previously stated, gathered the data, and not interpret it properly. The details tell the true story. The skill of communication is highly sought in the marketplace. We place a premium on it, but most of the time we only get half of what we pay for. What I mean by this is we are well versed in conveying our ideas and articulating our messages. Where we fail is in listening. Listening is more important when it comes to communicating. In his book, "The Seven Habits of Highly Effective People," Stephen Covey teaches us "to seek first to understand, then, to be understood." This is what effective communication is all about. Most of us spend too much time talking to understand what's being communicated.

Know your expectations early. Sometimes we will attempt to play shy and coy with our intentions. It is better to be upfront with your plans and give someone the opportunity to prove their honesty, and respond to your requirements. Setting expectations saves time and allows you to move at a swifter pace (If that's your goal). In the case of marriage, don't go in blind. You should seek the most intense marital counseling, not counseling "lite." Before you're at the point of no return (wherever that point is) discuss spending habits, credit reports, family medical history (including mental) and child rearing. Have a vision before you start traveling the marital highway. You can go nowhere fast.

Graceland

Walking down Beale Street in Memphis, Tennessee is quite the experience for a lover of the great music and food. Memphis boasts some of the best BBQ joints in the country and is home to many Blues artists. My first time visiting this great city was right before I got married. Both my mother-in-law and father-in-law were born in Memphis. Dad, my wife, brother-in-law, and sister-in-law all went to the University of Memphis, so they had deep roots in this city.

I was nervous when I asked Dad (my father in-law) for my wife's hand in marriage. I was giving someone my commitment to handle their prized possession responsibly. This commitment is not dependent on how that prized possession treated me. It's not reliant on all my needs being met; not on carnal desires, but on the premise "until death do we part." This is not a vow to be taken lightly. Just as my commitment to my father-in-law came with no strings attached, the expectation on my wife's part was just as high. I traveled all this way to ask for her hand.

I didn't know what to expect from this retired O.G. Air Force officer who I now call "Dad." He sized me up over the time of our courtship and was satisfied I would take great care of her. He did not mind me stealing his little girl. Now, I didn't have to get his blessing. This was an O.G. – Obtaining Greatness move.

Today, such old-school practice just isn't commonplace. But I believe there is something special about having the "blessing" of a father in marriage or going through proper protocol in any endeavor. This will give you something extra. It may not be tangible but it goes a long way. Here is a man who at that time had been married over 40 years and I wanted some of that wisdom! Over the time we spent together, before and even after Traci and I were married, Dad had lots of advice to share.

Then the LORD God made a woman from the rib he had taken out of the man, and he brought her to the man.
Genesis 2:22

How many times have you rolled over to your spouse and thought to yourself, "Lord what have I done?" That question does not dictate whether you love your spouse or not, it only shows the humanity that is in the similar challenges we face.

Rib Tips

- Love your spouse through the language he or she is fluent in. Your love language is for you.
- Be proactive in growing your marriage. Don't wait, always progress.
- After God, your marriage comes first. Not your kids, not your mamma or your daddy.
- Love unconditionally. Extend your spouse the grace to be human. Marriage is the land of "grace." Let that be your expectation.
- Marriage is about sacrificing one to another. It's not always fifty-fifty sometimes it could be ninety-nine to one.

For the Allocation Law to work in your marriage, we must make sure to rebalance whenever something gets past our limits, or the variance of what's acceptable and what's not. Rebalancing should be systematic with the understanding nothing will stay perfectly balanced. The key is to remain in harmony. Spouse, kids, work, or church will not have their specific allocated time from day to day. Life is too volatile for perfect allocation all the time. With harmony, we understand the vicissitudes of life will come and go throughout and our job is to enjoy the ride knowing there will be ups and downs. Over time, however, we will always win. Do you give the Allocation Law enough time to rebalance itself or are you always meddling?

The <u>uninformed</u> investor, over a twenty-year period, will probably gain less than five percent in the stock market. Unfortunately, we are not as disciplined as we should be. We are in and out of the market, by choice, at the worse possible times. When everything is flying high, and there's this feeling of I can't lose, we gamble and go all in. This is where we should take some of our profit off the table.

In our marriages, we get comfortable. You are uninformed regarding your spouse. You are working, the money is flowing. The kids are great, and we can start taking each other for granted which can set your marriage up for trouble. Don't take this as a time to relax and coast. This is a place to take your relationship to a whole new level. Take some profit!

Likewise, when fear hits the market, and values are down, we get very fearful and look to sell. The wise investor knows this is where you will find your best opportunities. If you didn't sell when your portfolio was worth more, why sell if it's worth less? If you hold quality securities, and you are not speculating or gambling, the best thing you can do is take your emotion out of it.

Does this mean you never cut your losses? No, but you don't go into marriage with an exit plan that is better thought out than the entrance plan. When you are going through tough times in your relationship and dealing with a setback you have the opportunity for the greatest comeback of all time!

Weeping may endure for a night, but joy comes in the morning. *Psalm 30:5*

Allow God to show himself mighty in your life during those tough times. Personally, I think I do pretty "good" on my own when all is well. Notice I said good. That's the level where my marital mishaps can be cured with a new pair of royal blue suede shoes (my wife's favorite color). On bad days, shoes don't cut it. If you have faith, throwing in the towel on your darkest days doesn't make sense. You will receive that two percent return life which isn't very good and definitely not O.G. This is the ultimate merger and acquisition. Make sure you walk in grace with one another.

The Smoke King

I am a black man. I never want to get to a point where I forget that, and then, I'm reminded by circumstance. It can be humbling and if you're not careful, fatal. From an O.G.'s perspective, your focus will be on thoughts that push you forward. We should focus on the goal. Focus where we want to go, and not someplace you don't want to be. An O.G. plays a potent offense. Don't misunderstand me, acknowledging your blackness is an offensive play. "Black" may seem risky, but no matter what history says, blackness encompasses the whole of all things beautiful, marriage included. "Black" is the ultimate allocation. It consists of the whole color spectrum and its power is undeniable. If you couldn't see it before, you should see it now.

I love to watch the interaction between Snoop Dogg and Martha Stewart on the cooking show "Potluck Dinner Party." Both unapologetically themselves, having a good time together. Each being their true selves while having fun and learning from one another. Allocation does not mean assimilation. Keep your flavor and enhance the atmosphere. Set the temperature instead of just measuring it. The color of smoke will vary from the blackest black to the whitest white. It is formless and expansive. It is a gas taking the shape of its container. This means you can be whomever and whatever you want to be. So, I ask you, what's stopping you from expanding? Rise as high as you desire and expand as wide as you wish. Only you can determine your dimensions. Whatever is weighing you down, drop it. No, in fact, drop it like it's hot. Where there's smoke, there is supposed to be fire. Where is your "fire?"

Hostile Takeovers

As an O.G., your strategy is a takeover. Don't think for one second what's rightfully yours, if in the hands of someone else, will be handed over nicely.

I've not gone all militant anti-law and order on you (if I were, it wouldn't be advertised in a book)! I am of the Gil Scott Heron mind. The revolution will not be televised, but it is internalized. What does this mean? The enemy of my enemy is my friend. I say "friend," the way Bishop TD Jakes describes "friend." His puts it like this.

Throughout your life you will associate with various people. You will have friends, confidants, and comrades. Real friends are your ride or die folk. They were with you in the beginning and they will be with you in the end. Good times and bad, sunshine and rain, you don't have to worry about these folks being in your corner. Next, you have your confidants. These people aren't necessarily for or against you, but they are for the things that you are for. You have a common goal, a common idea or value. Your interests align for the time being. There will be people in your life that don't like you. Your comrades don't like you, but they also don't like what you don't like. Sometimes you will need a common strategy to defeat a common enemy. After the conquest, you can go back to fighting each other.

Some fights are not to be fought alone. Some enemies have more might then you and your crew. These enemies are brought down strategically but, remember, hope is not a strategy. If you are hoping someone or something stops beating you upside your head, your "hope alone" methodology will probably insight them to beat even harder. Think of opportunities where it would be advantageous to join forces with other entities.

Divide and conquer is one of the oldest strategies in the book and it can only be nullified by unity. Fighting strategically allows the "Big Mo" to operate your life. Momentum makes a huge difference. Only then, will battles began to fall in your favor and the tide of the war changes. If you are not aligned in a unified direction, you will continue to be outflanked and outmaneuvered. You will keep your one step forward, two steps backward advances, and be fooled to believe your steps ahead are working. You will almost forget you are backtracking half of the time.

Private Equity

Not all fights are fought on the battlefield. When you announce your every move, and make known your plans, you've increased the resistance that will come against you. You give your opposition time to formulate contingency defense and preparation to your offensive drives. When you are in the public eye, all your operating information is open. Instead of having closed books, you are operating with a level of transparency that is only beneficial if you are working on a level playing field. Sometimes the strategy should bring everyone inside, no outsiders, strengthen our company to the degree that we become winners again, and when the time is right, reemerged as a public entity. Some problems lie solely with the management. That is, the leadership that is in charge should be held accountable or replaced. Whether it's your team, your family or your crew, the objective should be to develop within. This must be ingrained within each member until we inherently reproduce ourselves, thus strengthening our culture.

In Part III, we will discuss how this works. What does an O.G. - Obtaining Greatness culture look like? Right now, we must deal with the areas where we have had ineffective management or the lack of effective leadership. Remember, there are no bad teams only weak leaders. Some things stay in the family, and remember, never side against the family. I can't stress how important it is for you, or "US," to do the work ourselves when it comes to our community. That is the way the O.G. - Obtaining Greatness mindset develops. It comes from within not from without; not from outside. No one gives it to you and the resistance has made you stronger.

Angel Investors

Have you ever experienced a situation in your life that you knew had to be divine intervention? Was it a near miss car accident or an actual accident where you walked away without a scratch? It's a beautiful thing when God's favor shines on us and we have those guardian angel experiences. Life often is that way and those types of experiences are right on time. The great thing about this is it doesn't cost you anything. A sincere sense of gratitude is expected, but not demanded.

An angel investor, on the other hand, is different. When I was a kid, I heard my elders say that "all money wasn't good money." At that time, I took that to mean drug money, stealing or something of the illegal nature. I now know they really meant watch the strings that are attached. Or, don't be "penny wise and pound foolish." With an angel investor the keyword is "investor." Many entrepreneurs have been stung by taking too many trips to the proverbial honey pot. They quickly give up control before their vision is even wholly birthed. Sometimes people will "give" you something for securing favors later. These are your "Angels of Light" types. The Allocation Law allows us to grow at a faster rate than we normally would, but I caution that all growth is not good growth.

In the book "Profit First" by Mike Michalowicz, the process of growth at any price is challenged and dissected to show how it can be contrary to the reason an entity exists, which is profit. Instead of "Revenue = Expenses + Profit," we start with the premise of profit; "Profit = Revenue – Expenses." Determine your gain up front. What has to happen for you to consider it successful? Most of the time our concept isn't proven. We just continue to throw massive amounts of money at something until it works, or doesn't. The Allocation Law is strategic. Within the overall strategy, there will be some tactical components.

The angels in my life haven't come in the form of investors, but in the senior leaders and advisors I've sought out in life. I've found that great people genuinely love helping others. These are the people you find volunteering in your community and serving as leaders for your local nonprofits. They have many times retired from successful careers and are by no means finished serving. Too many times this group is overlooked as potential members of your crew. Just think about it. We measure wealth in time not just dollars and cents. So that man or woman who has served to the point of regaining and owning their time is wealthy. It's great to have wealthy people on your team. They are all around, but you must learn to recognize them as such. If they are not on your team, it's probably because you have not asked.

O.G. Code - Re-up

Acknowledge the brilliance, energy, and wisdom in people who are different from you. This can be very profitable. Wealth is not measured just in money. There is a level of class and distinction needed to understand this. An O.G. has these attributes. At this level, "I need you" is not a phrase uttered by the "dependent," but this is said by the "interdependent" also. Those who understand, know the mission is far greater than what they can accomplish alone.

- Recognize the strengths of other people and groups. These are the very areas you may be weak in. You will need to master this for Part III.
- Rethink the biases and prejudices you hold. We all have them, but we don't all acknowledge them. What is this keeping you from?
- Relive your life through the eyes and experiences of someone else. Empathy is very powerful and can allow you to see what you couldn't before.
- Recommit to your partner by perhaps renewing your marriage vows. Every five years make it a point to take an extra special vacation and indulge.
- Revive your spirit. Allow yourself to experience God on a new level by spending quality time in thoughtful study and meditation.
- Realign your relationships so they are a win for everyone. We all have strengths and weaknesses we can complement and enhance. If it doesn't work, don't be afraid to walk away.
- Replay every night before you go to bed and when you get up in the morning name a priority you want to accomplish. Go over each detail in your mind. Your subconscious will work on this when you are sleeping and you will reinforce this gameplay as you start your day.
- Rebalance your life. This is for harmony and not necessarily equality. There are seasons in your life when different areas will be prioritized. Understand the season you're in.
- Respect culture. Travel the world and actively seek people who are different from you. If you're not able to travel outside of your country, visit an ethnic neighborhood. The culture

you create goes deeper than just ethnicity. You want your values and belief system to be congruent with the legacy you want to leave.

- Revise your belief systems if they don't reflect where you want to go. As you get better information you will make better decisions. Decide how to allocate your resources in a way that will mitigate risk. People are your greatest resource.

Conclusion

The Allocation Law focuses on synergy. Synergy is created when the total equals more than the sum of the parts. This is not an occasional event. In every area of our lives, we want to be able to work together for the benefit of all concerned. Not only can you do more with others than what you can do alone, but the outcome is more significant in aggregate. This must become a lifestyle to live the O.G. - Obtaining Greatness way. Two plus two must equal five or more. Remember, mindset. When we change how we think and challenge some of the limiting beliefs we've held for so long, quantum events will begin to take place in our lives. It's like you lived a two-dimensional life and now we are adding more perspective, allowing you to see and experience what you never had before. It is in this space where creativity and innovation take place. In the next chapter, we will explore what this means for our communities and O.G.- Obtaining Greatness living at its finest.

Never be limited by other people's limited imaginations.

— *Dr. Mae Jemison*

Chapter X - Analyst and Alchemist
The Culture Law
By design or by default

Self-sufficiency or dependency? You can take what happens to you, or you can create what happens to you.

Creative Destruction

Do you remember your first job? You've just graduated from college. You are excited to become a productive member of an organization that will allow you to exercise your creative ability. You arrive at your office on your first day along with the other new recruits ready for orientation. After the human resource personnel goes over company policy and your benefits package, the vice president of your department steps up to speak. He references the fact that you, along with your colleagues, are the best and brightest. You've been selected because of your academic rigor and personal qualifications. He goes on to tell you, everything you've learned to this point, I need you to throw it out of the window. Forget the academics, forget the theory. We are going to show you how to be successful. Was the time you spent in the university library, the money you spent on four years of higher education, and the last four years of your time a waste?

I remember when my wife and I first married. Because we were married later in life, we had accumulated quite a bit of stuff. Well, my wife had collected a lot more than I had, but I think men and women are different in this way. Getting married later in life, also allowed us to come into the marriage more set in our ways than if we had married in our twenties. Rather than sift through all of our old stuff, and all of our old ideas, and everything that we learned from our parents, we found the ideal thing to do was to start over. Build from the perspective of what works for us. We tore down everything to build a stronger, more functional relationship for where we were in our lives. In the end, we still ended up with quite a bit of the stuff from before along with the wisdom, knowledge and understanding we learned from our parents. It was just structured in a way where the culture was our own and it worked for us. Just like what worked for our parents, worked for them.

Sometimes the most timely and effective way to build up is to tear down. You may keep the frame and the foundation but forget about how the walls and all the other aesthetics looked beforehand. A new hire may find that real-world experience is different from academia. A newlywed couple can thrive in building their relationship when they are creating new from the ground up, not with old building materials from past relationships. This is where putting in the time at the beginning, will reap dividends and time saved as you go forward.

It always amazed me whenever I watched one of those house flipping shows. Where you and I could only see an old rundown house, they can see a masterpiece. This is a real example of beginning with the end in mind. What happens when a company that has a culture of honesty, integrity and hard work merges with the company without those qualities? I'm sure you can picture in your mind what will happen in the long run. If no changes are made in personnel, with an emphasis on what we want our culture to look like, it won't be pretty.

Starting from the beginning and starting new can save a lot of time when the goal is the creation. Creation is a significant part of O.G. - Obtaining Greatness culture. Creators take their destiny into their own hands, and this allows them to fulfill their vision and leave a legacy. Many people in life will talk a good game, but when it's time to create they fall short. If you spend all your time talking and very little of your time doing, sooner or later, you will notice everyone around you progressing while you complain about everything that is wrong in your life. If this is you, I suggest you revisit Part I and take ownership so you can see that change is up to you. Everyone in your crew must understand this. It must be something on the inside of them that directs all choices and decisions accordingly. Everyone on your team should buy into this.

This principle comes into play when we talk about the speed of trust. It also comes into play when we speak of the total being more significant than the sum of the parts. The Culture Law takes us from "place" to "position." Place represents the past, what we were and any problems we've had. You can encounter people from your past and there's friction because you are not in the same "place" you were the last time you both met. "Position" changes this by adding direction. That direction is toward your legacy. Now, you have the velocity to get there. Before, you were aimlessly wandering. You build in the right direction one brick at a time. The Culture Law will fast-track our legacy. This seems like a tall order, and you might not feel it is possible. Let's look within and see why we think this way.

Internal Dialogue

Our collective self-talk, as a community, has consisted of so many voices saying so many different things it's a wonder anything gets done. Most of the voices contradict each other or weigh heavily on the side of the negative. The easiest thing to do is to sit back and complain. We were taught as children if you couldn't say something nice to say nothing. I would like to expand on this. If what you are saying does not add a solution to the problem, or if it doesn't edify or enhance the conversation, say nothing. This works only to the extent we are wearing our public faces. What happens when we are behind closed doors talking amongst ourselves? A negative vibe can quickly grow into mutiny, and in doing so, start sowing seeds of destruction and dissension. This destruction is not the general calamity type but damaging enough to shift us into an unproductive mood. If you stay in this mood long enough, you start to see it reflected in your everyday conduct and conversation. Before long the constant division will keep you from making any forward progress. Have you checked your group talk lately? Group talk can develop around a topic you may or may not believe in, and if analyzed by truth, would not even stand merit. Depending on the community you live in, group talk could go something like this.

"All of the foreigners are taking our jobs."
"The government continues to oppress the people."
"We need to raise the minimum wage."
"We don't need to raise the minimum wage."

None of this is O.G. – Obtaining Greatness. In fact, it barely scrapes the surface of "good." I would say you're probably dealing with average people and you need to reassess who you are connected to.

But God...

More than any other time in history the tools for creation have been placed in our hands. This is a godsend. Can you imagine what it would take for you to produce YouTube shows you enjoy now over twenty years ago? It would be next to impossible without big money and connections. I think technology is God's way to bless his people. Before you start ranting about the evils of cell phones and social media, I challenge you to think differently. It's like money. You've probably heard the scripture misquoted, "Money is the root of all evil." To correct this, it's the "love" of money. Money is a tool, neither good nor bad; it's amoral. The value is in how you use it.

The same can be said with technology. While we can agree social media, cell phones, and most things digital have shortened the attention spans of millions, there are many social benefits with millions of dollars being made. The question is which side of the money equation are you going to play on? Not only does the O.G. recognize when he or she is getting played, but the O.G. also recognizes an opportunity. The internet spells opportunity. God is not anti-social media. What can you create out of this? That should be the question asked whenever something "different" crosses our paths.

Far too often we condemn what we don't understand, and sometimes back it up with "God said..." The sad thing is we pass down this way of thinking to our children. Then they grow up not fully understanding the creative power of God and how we are to emulate Him. It's time to stop looking at God as our genie in a bottle that we can rub from time to time and make something happen.

We justify unanswered prayers as "not in God's timing" when all along He is telling us to use what's in our hand to create anything we want. When you imagine, then attempt to build what you saw in your imagination, God will fill in the blanks when you run into difficulties. This is the "those that help themselves" part of the saying God helps those who help themselves. I heard someone say, "God responds to seeds not needs." Let me add that when I say "seed," I'm not just thinking of tithes or money. In this case, I challenge you to consider how you manage the other ninety percent as testament to you being a good steward of God's blessing in your life, or not. It's what we do with what's in our hand. God has placed creative genius in each of us, and like any other muscle, if it's not exercised, it will atrophy.

You have let your imagination lay dormant for too long, and now is the time to resurrect it! You must change your mindset to tap into this, and I know you can because you've made it this far in this book. If you didn't believe that mindset was everything then you would have laid this book down a long time ago. How do we exercise our imagination and get back to that creative god-like spirit? Here are a few things you should consider.

- Challenge old mindsets and preconceived ideas. Don't accept those ideas that put the responsibility outside of you or plans which allow you to be victimized.
- Practice visualization by holding the thought of what you desire in your mind. As you work your imagination muscle it will become stronger. The same is true for your doubts, so dismiss anything contrary that comes to mind.
- Study scripture that speaks of building, creating, accomplishing, or stewardship. A balanced diet will allow you to grow stronger and fewer sweets will benefit you long-term. Don't get addicted to the "pie in the sky" when you can have the "veggies of victory" right now.
- Teach your children to be interdependent and self-sufficient. They are going to do exactly what they see you do and that becomes our culture.

Looking at ourselves will allow change to take place. Pointing the finger at others does not effect change. Understand there is enough of everything to go around. When you are creative there is no lack. When everyone is creative we develop a no lack mentality and culture. How wonderful would that be? Before we can get there, we first need to address a few more mindsets and institutions that can't be ignored.

The Critical Element

Revolutionaries are one hundred percent anti-establishment. They will find something wrong in every institution or organization that our country has been established upon. Now, I'm not saying many of those institutions or establishments shouldn't be critiqued or even destroyed, but there is no patience in the revolutionary. He believes now is the time! I understand waiting won't help. The problem with the revolutionary is that although their boldness and ferocity is to be admired, the revolutionary is ill equipped and hasn't thought out an implementable strategy. In essence, he brings a knife to a gun fight. What I mean by this, is that we have not yet acquired any tools of production, let alone the weapons of war; and by weapons, I mean political, economic, or social.

Political weapons include everybody voting. This is something that is in your control. Low voter turnout is rampant in our community and we need to change this. There is a bad mindset that says, "My vote doesn't matter." This will get you killed. Don't draw your gun before it's loaded. Learn to shoot. Don't shoot yourself in the foot. When you don't vote, this is exactly what you are doing.

The revolutionary will point out the fact that failed policies, political and economic disenfranchisement, and a host of other situations, stop us from obtaining greatness. They have a very valid point, but again, if we misdirect our energies we will come up short. What would happen if you had to wait until an injustice was corrected before you could be an O.G.? I am in many ways, anti-establishment. When we begin to be revolutionary within our communities, it will start to affect the culture. The revolution will not be televised, but it must be internalized.

Status quo people are even more dangerous than the revolutionaries. By their very nature, they play into the hands of any forces benefiting from the stagnation in our community. They attempt to play both sides. They are split between those who are raging against the system just enough to show their disdain all while profiting from said system. Then, they will look past the support needed for the "least of these" who would need the most help.

Status quo people take up a lot of space. It's important to understand again that greatness is a mindset. It is not a political affiliation. It is not social, economic status. These are tools to be used and it's only when you change your mindset do you see things differently. Status quo people will see everything that is wrong, but their actions will rarely rise to the level needed to make an impact.

O.G. – Obtaining Greatness culture is revolutionary. You should think differently, move differently, and behave differently than you have ever before. Although it may seem counterintuitive, it is our intuitive cultural conditioning that has us where we are now in the first place, good or bad. It's one thing to behave this way as an individual, it's another to lead your family or to lead your team to do the same. The reconnaissance has been done, and this is the strategy we need to follow; first inside, then out. This is the strategy that will work for you personally, for our families, and for our community. No one is going to give it to you. You will have to fight, and if you want to fight, put the knives away. You're fighting an enemy that's using deadly weapons. Your lethal weapon is your mindset.

You're so close!

I have a friend who takes his family camping every year. His wife doesn't like camping. Actually, she hates it. She does understand the life skills and lessons afforded to her children, and enjoyment for her husband. Every year, he promised his wife they will have more fun this year than the year before. Each year, his wife reluctantly went but hated it. His wife continued in the same illusion for about four years. She lived with this anguish until last year's vacation when she discovered that the campground they had been visiting for years, was only twenty minutes from a massive shopping complex. It had all the creature comforts she expected for a vacation get-a-way. Now, she spends a considerable amount of time shopping when they vacation.

What if I told you that everything you have been promised, but have not received yet, could be had with just a change of focus? I know I would get the "side eye" from most people in the struggle because you've worked all your life and nothing around you resembles the promised land. I understand walking for forty years for a three days' journey. I challenge you to recognize what is close within your reach, or just beyond. Sometimes we look too far into the future for change and abundance.

That inner-city property you've owned, and are now willing to sell for little or nothing, will in ten years be redeveloped into million-dollar condominiums. That idea you've had for a unique eatery will jump from your head into someone else's if you don't act on it. No, none of this will happened overnight. You will need to put in the work. It seems like it was overnight when you opened your eyes one day and see entire blocks transformed in your community. Or, perhaps, read about your idea in the Wall Street Journal. The wilderness can blind you to the nearby opportunities. If only we practiced acting more than talking, we could save ourselves. What is your wilderness experience? What inaction will you pass down to the next generation? What ideas are your children inheriting, or not? The following will address two areas where we (your team, crew, family, etc.) have been walking in circles.

Generational curses - I was a single parent. My mother was a single parent. Her father was a single parent. Although each of the circumstances were very different, this is an area in my life, and the lives of many of my family members, that need continued vigilance. Very different circumstances with the same exact outcome. It's easy to ignore and chalk it up to coincidence. In fact, nobody in my family recognizes or talks about it. It will save the next generation a lot of heartbreak, and despair, if we fully deal with it on a mental, emotional, and spiritual level. Or, around the woods, we go.

Mental illness - This is a taboo subject in our community because of the stigma attached. Priority and resources placed on treating this condition in our society is lacking. According to the National Network of Depression Centers, one out of five Americans suffer from depression. It is the number one cause of disability in people ages 15-44. When I was younger, we threw the word "crazy" around a lot. This is unfortunate and reinforced the stigma. It is vital for family and friends to reach out to those who may be suffering from depression, or any mental illness. Showing you are there for support is very helpful. Don't allow a judgmental, or "let me fix you," attitude hinder genuine support. Just be there.

A wilderness "experience" versus "wilderness living" is different. When you experience it then you acknowledge it early on. This doesn't mean it's corrected right away, but awareness is critical. The longer you continue in this direction without awareness, it stops being just an experience and turns into a way of life. Being creative in this state is tough. You will likely paint the world a dark picture and draw others to you that will help develop this portrait. The old saying "misery loves company" can manifest as a life of living in the wilderness.

The Complain Lane

Sometimes as a group we don't recognize the wilderness. It's not so bad when all your family and friends are there with you, or so it seems. Creativity is the fast lane on a highway that is congested with everyone's opinion and critique. We're stuck in traffic. Even though the fast lane is open, there are few who decide to travel it. "Stuck" is comfortable. You don't have to move, or grow, or decide. You are where you are, and because you are with your friends, or family, or people who think like you, it's ok.

I believe when our public-school system cuts extracurricular activities the creative spirit is hindered. If you keep on doing what you're doing, you'll keep on getting what you have been getting. Sometimes you get unstuck for a while and you equate this with progress. This on again off again, it's like a relationship. It's predictable and you never accomplish your goal of marriage, family or, just being your best self.

Creativity puts you in a spiritual flow that seems to transcend time. This flow is important when accomplishing anything as a team. Everyone's game is on point and we're hitting shot after shot. How do we get out of the "complain lane" when the negative opinions of others congest our life's road?

Objects in mirror are closer than they appear

When you look at someone do you see their negative tendencies and flaws? What is it about that person who just gets on your last nerve? Or, do you find the best in them? Most of the time what we see in others, can reflect our own issues. They become the mirror for a deep dive into our psyche, and the areas we wish we could change or areas that challenge us. Knowing your "place" and "position" are vital in changing lanes. Location is where you are currently and home is where you want to go. It's just like your "place" and "position." If you don't address these areas they will eventually become blind spots in your life. The journey will take longer. As a leader, you want an accurate assessment of yourself, and the progress you are making with your team.

Blinkers

How do you communicate to others you're about to make a change? I always tell my children, "It's not always what you say, but what you do that counts." If you are in your car traveling at any rate of speed you can say, or even yell, your intentions all day long and no one would be any wiser. Others going with you may have also seen you do this before. Until you make an action that shows you are doing something differently, your words will only frustrate those who rely upon them for direction.

Your blinkers are a visual that give clues to those around you about the direction you are headed. If it is a change of direction for your health the blinker may be a change in the groceries you bring into your home. There will be fewer chips and dip but more fruit and vegetables.

If it is something specific to a negative attitude, our blinker may involve someone holding you accountable and challenging you on your negative self-talk. Or, use a swear jar. Make noncompliance cost you something. Blinkers can be subtle or they can be blaring. The important thing is they are actions that will show others how to, and how not to, interact with you. People will ignore what you say if there's no corresponding actions. You are teaching them how to respond to you.

Speed limits

The movement of an organization will be limited by the level of trust between the people and the size of that organization. Sports cars accelerate faster than semi-trucks. You may be the in the cab of a semi-truck as a leader, but don't forget about the trailer you have behind you. The "speed of trust" will allow you to travel at a safe speed for your vehicle. Don't ask your passengers to do something you wouldn't do. If you are not comfortable changing lanes at 85 mph then don't ask anyone else to do so.

When changing the culture of an organization, it is a prolonged and deliberate process. You did not get to this place overnight, and it is entirely possible your journey will include some rest stops. If you have a mechanical problem with your vehicle, meaning an organizational issue, you should probably travel at a speed lower than what is posted until it is resolved. You may even need to find the nearest exit to stop and fix the problem. It is cheaper to stop the production line and make the corrections than it is to recall faulty products later.

Rearview

When you are driving, most of your time will be spent going forward. Rarely are you driving in "reverse" for any length of time. A creative culture should allow time for reflection. Don't confuse this time with dwelling on the past. Instead, it is an opportunity to gauge progress. Make sure you are headed in the right direction. I like to use the acronym "P.L.A.N." The 'P' represents your Position, 'L' your Legacy or destination, 'A' the Action steps followed to get there and 'N' are your Notes or points of interest along the way.

The problem arises when we confuse the 'P.' We substitute 'Place' for "Position." 'Place' is where you have been prior to starting your journey. It represents where we are leaving. This is your pre-self-awareness status. If you're not aware, you will not go in the right direction. We want to get away from our old self and grow into our legacy. The 'P' in the "P.L.A.N." acronym stands for Position. The difference between Place and Position is direction. Once we are "positioned" toward our 'L' or legacy, at any point in time, we may get off track. Using our rearview as a tool to see the last instruction completed keeps us from attempting to go back to our former 'Place.' We reposition as needed. In Maxwell Maltz's book "Psycho Cybernetics" this is called the "Servo mechanism." Most the time you might be a little off course, but through many micro corrections, we make it to our destination. Those corrections equate to how we handle our problems in life.

Our 'L' or legacy is secured through correction. How do we know if we get off track? Your 'A', or "action," is compared to your 'N', your "notes." This is where the "S.M.A.R.T.O.G." helps your short-term goals build into your mid-range, then eventually your long-term, or legacy. It's imperative that your "notes," your 'N,' are written down. If you don't write it down you have nothing to compare and measure your actions by. This will keep you off course. You will end up going where you didn't want to go, staying longer than you wanted to stay, and doing what you didn't want to do. Write it down.

A creative culture leads us to a culture of self-sufficiency and self-determination. This is the O.G. - Obtaining Greatness culture. The Culture Law causes us to analyze ourselves and the behaviors that have gotten us to this point in our lives. We examine what it will take to get to our destiny. That destiny is one of perpetual excellence where we actively create the legacy we want to leave to our children. Self-reflection and analysis is part of the long game. God has put eternity in the hearts of men. You won't see the end, but you are establishing a foundation for your children. You create this foundation and no one else. You create on the macro and micro level. It's important to know where to critique or analyze and where to design, build up, or make from scratch what is missing or underdeveloped.

189

O.G. Code - Culture Club

Constructive criticism is vital for growth. If we don't like to listen to the critiques of others, then we must be the first ones to critique ourselves. Even then, you don't have the proper objective vantage point to see everything. This is medicine for the creative soul. The creative spirit in you can only flourish when you accept dominion over self and take it out of the hands of others. You have the power to soar. The question is how high do you want to fly?

- Self-examination will take you ten times further then attempting to make someone else see his or her flaws. Don't waste your energy.
- Don't discuss problems without solutions. This is equivalent to complaining although we may justify it as an activity that needs our attention. Stay solution minded.
- As you are solution minded, remember to build trust and buy-in from your team. Know when you need to run and when to walk. Pay attention to the speed limits.
- Complaining sows discord in your organization. Address concerns with decisive action. Don't allow this to fester and grow.
- Allow your people the opportunity to think differently. Status quo thinking will not solve status quo problems. You must think on a higher level.
- As you open your mind to higher level thinking your creativity will increase. Become comfortable in this space and encourage it throughout your organization.
- Creativity will allow God to demonstrate His power in your life. You will never have all the answers. That should not hinder you from stepping out and doing things differently.

- Exercise your imagination. Know what you don't know, and try imagining solutions. Brainstorm. The default is to think it can't be done or the problem can't be solved.
- Don't impose your limitations on your children. Don't let them complain, but allow them to explore their dissatisfaction to the point of creating a solution.
- You are a creator. It's in your DNA as a child of the Most High God. Lack of faith can equate to a lack of creative genius being exhibited. We have all been given a measure of creative genius. Exercise your faith.

Conclusion

Webster defines culture as "the integrated pattern of human knowledge, belief, and behavior that depends upon the capacity for learning and transmitting knowledge to succeeding generations." Parts I and II of this book focused on developing and expanding that capacity. Now, we will take that "integrated pattern" and apply it in a fashion that will affect the generation of you the reader, and as stated in Psalms13:22 "A good man leaves an inheritance to his children's children...." This is O.G. - Obtaining Greatness. It is a lifestyle for you, and culture for our community. We are done with "You," you understand the power of your "Crew" and now it's time to focus on how we impact generations to come by building community.

Part III - Manifesto

For the Community

There is more untapped potential in the Black community than anywhere else

There is a higher value on what's in your hand

Govern your community to your advantage, put your interest first

The greatest intellectual property stays in the community

The greatest businessmen are in your community

You are prepared with talents that can't be learned in school

Violence has no place in our community

Your service protects the community

People are your greatest resource

Your legacy will be one of transformation

Chapter XI - The Greater Society
The Possibility Law
Appreciate what you have, go out and get more

Gratitude gives you material to make something out of nothing. The intangibles you don't see with your natural eye are game changing.

The Great Creators

For some folks, it's far-fetched to believe that culture is created by following the laws of Part I and Part II of this book, but what if it is? Remember, change your mindset, change your life! What if this O.G. – Obtaining Greatness experiment produced something far different from what we are experiencing now? Even though it may not be perfect, would you embrace it? These are some of the questions asked when we explore The Possibility Law.

The Possibility Law could also be called the act of being open-minded. If you have a closed mind, or a fixed mindset, as discussed in Part I of this book, your reality is limited and change is out of your control. With an open mindset, the world is yours. This is where the attitude of gratitude, and thanking Him in advance, allows you to continue flowing in your "zone." All things are possible to him who believes!

To walk in the Possibility Law, you must accept there is an answer to your dilemma and the answer is within your reach right now! Once you have mastered yourself and you learn to interact with others O.G. culture is yours for the asking. It's a faith walk, and at the same time continuous work. We want to live "that life." "That life" is the one we fell away from and are now ready to reconnect to. "That life" doesn't take no for an answer. You do whatever it takes; the real ones are separated from the fake ones.

The Possibility Law is based on a quote by Napoleon Hill which says, "Whatever the mind can conceive, and believe, it will achieve." We're taught at an early age to repress our imaginations and this is unfortunate. It inhibits our innovation and creativity. You can't change your current level of problems with the same level of thinking used to create them.

This is not wishful thinking that I propose but a vision to embrace your higher self and release the God-given gifts and talents that are within. Gifts and talents that contain every answer to all your problems. First, accept that you are great; right where you stand. No one will develop your product for you. In this marketplace, everyone should come with something in their hand. Something to sell, to trade or value to deliver in some way.

This is the game. Do some people cheat? Absolutely! That's just a character flaw. Cheaters don't win the long game, but they will win against someone who doesn't know a game is being played. Or, anyone who refuses to even learn the rules. You don't know if you're being cheated on, or not, if you don't know the rules. Your default way of thinking is that everyone is deceiving you. We miss our shot and instinctively cry foul. You know the referees won't get every call right. That doesn't matter to a winner. You continue to play hard. You continue to develop. You continue to win, and figure out what you can do differently next time if you lose.

This is the O.G. - Obtaining Greatness mindset. You're grateful to be in the game and sometimes you'll even play hurt. Pain is a part of the game. It's a constant that will continue, so stop crying about it. Please don't debate me on this, just accept it. This may seem unfair, but what happens when a generation of people think like this? They pass it on to their children.

A Nation of Millions

How do we sell this mindset? You don't need to sell it. Gratefulness at this level you either have it or you don't. You can tell those who do. It gives you a higher level of resourcefulness. If you ever find yourself disadvantaged, gratitude causes you to elevate above your circumstances and find a way, somehow. Ungrateful people feel hopeless. This sense of hopelessness can and will become the defining mindset of a generation then, their offspring. Likewise, nothing can hold back a society willing to embrace their creative genius, and solve problems through a collective effort, and self-reliance.

I'm personally grateful for some of the revelations brought about by the current political climate. I must admit, I fell asleep at the wheel and thought social conditions had improved in America beyond their actual state. I like keeping that type of reality right in front of my face knowing I have what it takes inside to combat any fight waged against me, strategically. The gratitude mindset forces you to look inward before looking outward.

An O.G. should recognize this as one of the most potent tactics of success. If you took the black pill back in chapter three, you will masterfully play the cards you've been dealt and you may possibly lose a hand. Again, this is chess not checkers. This only puts you in position to grow sharper. If you spend all your time trying to change the nature of your opponent, you make a lot of noise, but you'll always lose.

An O.G. has what it takes to win. That includes a spirit of gratefulness. A winner's mindset won't allow for excuses, complaints or worry about the opposition. Again, it's the difference between the great and mediocre. If I can force you into mediocrity, I know all your efforts to compete with me will fall short. You will get more of what you focus on. If you focus on what's wrong with the world, don't be surprised to receive more of those same circumstances.

Throughout this book, we have talked about the importance of having the right mindset. No one will agree on everything at the micro level but having a macro alignment of essential ideas and attitudes will lead us to a place we haven't seen before. The oldest trick in the book has been to divide and conquer. This tactic crosses all racial, political and socio-economic lines. Some people know that unity is a force to be reckoned with and a united front is next to impossible to defeat.

We need the collective mindset that says "anything" is possible. Once we buy into this we get to decide what that "anything" will be. Collective greatness will be a sight to behold and the impact will be generational. This is the point we move from scarcity to abundance. Everybody eats, and everybody's needs are met, because everybody contributes. Remember, if you think you can or think you can't, either way, you're right.

Exceedingly, Abundantly, above all...

When I was a kid, I remember a gospel song that would play in our home and the chorus simply said, "Be Grateful." The choir was very melodic in how they sang those two words to the point it left an indelible mark on my childhood memories. When I listened to the song recently, it elicited a feeling of joy over just how far I had come in life and my outlook on what's to come. That song reminded me of my mindset of scarcity then versus my mindset of abundance now.

To the O.G., opportunity becomes a commodity. I share this belief with my children and it's increased the capacity of my family 1,000-fold. Their perceived limitations, shortcomings and mistakes are no match for the possibility they feel is within their grasp. I'm okay with knowing some of the vision I have for my family will come to pass after I'm long gone. It will be the role of my grandchildren, great-grandchildren and their children, and there will be plenty of whatever they need available to get the job done.

"Buy real estate because God's not making any more of it." This is a saying I would sometimes hear from investors. They would also complain about the market's being overbought, oversold, or have various excuses of why now isn't a good time. Or, why we may have missed the best time and timing is everything. The O.G.'s perspective is always different.

We haven't begun to master cultivating all that's available to us here on earth. By cultivating, I don't mean "use up" but enjoy, replenish or enhance. Yet, there are those who are already looking past earth towards the next frontier of space exploration. I said next because to an O.G. it's never final.

I'm really stretching your faith now, but this should put some of your perceived limitations in perspective. You might say, "Space exploration, really?" Ask Jeff Bezos, Richard Branson or Elon Musk. O.G., you're thinking Amazon, Virgin and Tesla. These guys are thinking Blue Origin, Galactic and SpaceX. Did our ancestors sail to the New World hundreds of years ago, or were they afraid of falling off the face of the earth? An O.G. thinks bigger and lives in the land of "more than enough." You eat very well and that does not stop me from eating.

Abundance thinking is an intangible product that once purchased, begins to provide many tangible benefits. You start to see in your life, your family's life and the community, benefits that will only manifest themselves in the spirit of cooperation and expectation. How do we tap into a sense of gratitude and abundance to understand possibility? Can you think your way happy?

What's your belief System?

If you have ever been involved in a network marketing venture, you know there is a point within your downline where your organization becomes self-sustaining. At this point, you have reached what's called "critical mass." You will grow beyond this point, but this is the level necessary to achieve sustainability. Network marketing works but it ultimately works for those who work it.

Why do I so adamantly attempt selling you this product called "possibility?" Because I am a dealer and this is my product. There must be enough people who not only believe in the product but also the opportunity. A negative belief system can become like an addictive drug. A meth dealer doesn't necessarily "sell" meth. They "offer" it and the addictive nature of the product takes care of itself. This negative force takes on a life of its own and affects negatively everything it touches. The key here is running from everything negative and embracing all things positive. Just like with cocaine and baking soda, or ephedrine and ammonia, there is a method to reaching positive critical mass in the nervous system of our society.

I believe I can fly

Do you remember when you were a child and you had these wild dreams of what you wanted to accomplish in life? There were dreams like being a great inventor, curing cancer or even being President of the United States. Somewhere between childhood and adolescence it seems as if aliens came to earth, stole our abilities and talents when it came to dreaming big. They took our belief and we lost our faith.

The greater society walks a journey built on what's possible and what you must do to make this possibility a reality. This is the framework on which the American dream was built. Please save

199

your discussion on if the American dream is achievable to everyone. No one is limited in, nor to, this country. To the O.G., the world is his or her oasis waiting for them to enjoy. This is the product that must be sold not only to our children but also every person who's waiting on a solution to whatever problem they are facing. There is a generation that will die in the wilderness. They will die malnourished because this self-sufficiency food is too hard to swallow. I challenge you to chew a little more on the O.G. – Obtaining Greatness philosophy, and it will over time, become more digestible, more natural to the palette and eventually desired. This delicacy is an acquired taste, but once you're hooked on it you can't have a meal without it.

So how do we buy into this thought of collective individualization? It sounds absurd, but the more I get my act together instead of imposing my will on you, the better we become. It's that synergy of two + two equaling five, or more. It's one putting one thousand to flight and two putting ten thousand to flight. If what you're doing now is working, continue. Our old belief system or habits must be replaced with something new that works for us. Remember, mindset. Now it's a global mindset.

Good Mentality

In chapter four we talked about "Good" being the enemy to the "Great." The "Good" mentality will cause you to accept living below your privilege. This is a trap of complacency and it causes us to grow accustomed to not innovating, creating or thinking for ourselves. The following three areas can affect us, but only one of them will allow you to escape this trap.

Goodies

Goodies are the delivered on promises of any and everyone who's provided help to you. You may not have needed it but were a beneficiary of the "gift" nonetheless. Goodies are never enough, in fact, they are rather insufficient to take care of your needs. It's easy to become reliant on this form of benevolence like anything else that takes the edge off life. But, it's the edge that fosters growth. So, after a while, you're not growing. Possibilities are diminished in a slow to no growth environment. You only see what you are given and, at most, what is promised to you but never delivered.

Paper Goods

Paper goods are temporal, disposable; promises that provide just enough hope to keep us running in place. We are moving but not advancing. The illusion caused by movement justifies our fatigue and weariness. "Surely, I'm doing something right," we tell ourselves. We dare not believe we've worked so hard, spent so much time and energy to earn a bill of goods that won't be delivered. Paper goods are extended by employers and agencies alike. The corporate ladder can be an example of a paper good, so can your 401K plan at work, or your social security plan. You are supposed to be able to retire, right? Are you still waiting for that legislation that will make all well? It will be as good as the paper it's written on or not written on. Honestly, paper goods will not be enough either. The paper goods do not amount to policy backed by due process. Here we are still trading for trinkets while being lead with bad policy.

"Can" goods

"Can" goods protect you in troubled times. We can eat during a famine or other natural disaster. Their long shelf-life allows us to weather storms if we take on an "I can" attitude. "Can" goods are important if you know there's work to be done after the storm; for a season, more work and harder work than before. It's amazing what we can accomplish with our backs against the wall. I wonder what would happen if we used those "can" goods all the time and replaced the goodies and paper goods?

"Can" goods provide options. They give you the possibility of a brighter future no matter what has happened in your life. They represent what can't be taken away, even with a fight. These are the containers that hold the ingredients you contribute to the American dream. Please understand this dream is big enough for everyone. When you internalize "more than enough," you move on to greater. The pie is big enough for everybody. Good becomes something we may occasionally fall back on if times are ever rough. Those times become fewer and farther between when you know that you "can."

A Good Piece of Pie

Life doesn't stop with appreciating what you have but it is foundational. Gratitude gives you the ability to go far beyond your current status. Remember, mindset. Would you choose to have 50 percent of an existing pie or 10 percent of a growing pie? Now, I can hear some of you asking, "How big is the pie?" In our quest for equality, the reality is all things are not equal nor will they ever be. Equality is a very simplistic answer to a very complex problem. Of course, everyone should be treated with fairness, honesty, and integrity. Instead the reality is we all have different gifts and abilities. We have different goals. We all have different drives and different levels of accomplishment. Focusing on how the pie is divided makes me put too much attention on your slice and not enough attention to what's on my plate. You are focusing on what is, as opposed to what is possible. Do you want to "move on up?" Or, do you want to just have "good times?"

When I was a kid one of my favorite television shows was "The

Jefferson's." One reason I like this show so much was the main character George Jefferson, played by the late Sherman Helmsley, was not afraid to speak his mind and took responsibility for his own welfare. More important than that, the show gave an image of possibility. This show changed the mindset of a young kid from what was birthed through my environment to a vision of what I wanted my future to look like. I knew what my reality was; I knew what that looked like. I was living that every day and did not need to hear or see more of the same. I'm from the "dirt" as some say. If where you come from is stopping you from going somewhere else, by all means forget where you came from; for a season. Do this to gain some traction in your life. Change your mindset, change your life.

Another show I loved growing up was "Good Times." Florida and James Evans were a hard working lower-middle-class couple who, for whatever reason, always struggled and barely made it. Focusing only on your current reality causes it to become more ingrained and you continue to get more of the same. We can continue to work hard and struggle to live for the weekend. These are the only days we see our "good times." Or, we can "move on up," as the chorus to the theme song on "The Jefferson's" says.

Sometimes we detach what we know is vital for our success from our everyday reality. For example, if you have read this far, you see the power of affirmations, vision boards and keeping your eyes focused on where you want to go, not where you are or where you have been. Don't focus on where you don't want to go. This is on a micro level. The micro should lead to a similar macro vision. Instead the macro view, in some of our communities, is the exact opposite.

The Possibility Law must be enforced to build a greater society. If we allow the media to paint and broadcast the vision then we are in trouble. Turn on any news broadcast and you will see just what I mean. How much of this can we digest as a society before it becomes a self-fulfilling prophecy? The same could probably be said for hip-hop culture. What you focus on, you become. Hip-hop culture must get back to its roots. I was raised on hip-hop and I credit some of my success to this movement. Leadership equals influence. Hip-hop culture is one of the most significant impacts on my generation. Where is hip-hop leading us? What is hip-hop influencing us to do today?

What you consistently tell yourself every day will affect your actions. Those actions become your habits and the habits become your character. Your character will lead to your destiny. I love how hip-hop expresses our need to have more, be more, and do more. It is a message that resonates with many that come from humble beginnings. Although music is a place where we get a lot of our inspiration, motivation, and drive to make money, it falls far short in its ability to develop men and women of character. Nor, I would argue, is it supposed to. Money without integrity is a disaster waiting to happen. The disaster might not hit you, but it will inevitably affect your children or even grandchildren.

An O.G. is interested in the long game. That game extends far beyond his or her lifetime. Healthy eating habits can take you further in life than more money. Likewise, your character enables you to solidify your succession plan. When it comes to money, we should understand the possibilities in this Internet age are abundant. I caution the reader when money is the primary objective and not a byproduct of your service.

I grew up listening to motivational speaker, Les Brown. Mr. Brown would always brag about his mother and her delicious sweet potato pies. I can't speak as good as Les Brown, but I will put my mother's sweet potato pies up against his mother's any day. My mother cooks one of the best sweet potato pies you would ever want to taste. She knows I love her sweet potato pies and will always have one ready for me when I come to visit. One day I noticed she had changed her recipe a bit. Instead of using the standard pan to bake her pies, she had switched to using a new deep dish pan. I love the texture of foods. When she made this change the pie was still great, but I had to adjust the size of my slice to get the pie and crust in the perfect proportions. Although I started eating smaller slices. there was just as much satisfaction and more pie to spare. How do we grow the pie for everyone? Is it possible to have the same size or an even smaller slice and be just as or even more, satisfied? The Possibility Law challenges us to go for "greater."

Richer Desserts

There is an old saying that says, "You can't have your cake and eat it too." One thing I loved more than my grandma's sweet potato pie was her chocolate cake. Her chocolate cake was like old money. She made them in layers. Three, four, sometimes even five layers of pure deliciousness. If a bigger slice of pie made you happy, the bigger slice of cake made you rich! The cake was like a compound blessing where, although you may have had the same size slice, the number of layers increased the magnitude.

When we have jobs in our community for the people that live there, it's like having a larger slice of pie, and that's good. But, when we own the means of production in our community, when we are more producer and less consumer, we then own the cake which we can layer as high as we want. That's great! A bigger pie might represent an increase in profits for the owners which may lead to an increased wage for the workers. It's two dimensional. Cake, on the other hand, is three-dimensional. It's vertically integrated. The vegetables you harvest from your farm are served to your neighbors who dine in your restaurant. The owners live in the community. Now, when you have an increase in income, you have an increase in profits, and those profits continue to turn over within our community. We want the cake! An O.G. must be aware and take advantage of all cake opportunities. By doing so, we never should worry about "bread." There is a difference between normal awareness and O.G. - Obtaining Greatness awareness. The Possibility Law is the lens you should use to see the world through.

When a real estate developer looks at a rundown, infested, old track of land many times, he sees something entirely different from the average person. This average person could have lived in this area for many years. They may have even seen the city in its former glory. Because of their familiarity, and the lack of perspective, they are unable to see the potential gold mine in their own backyard. Sometimes we are too close to what could possibly bless us the most. We sell for pennies on the dollar items that make other people fortunes. We pay top dollar for depreciating assets. Change your mindset, change your life.

The Possibility Law makes you exercise your imagination. Step way back, far enough to get a change in perspective. Are there growth possibilities here? If so, where can I add value? Where is the best return on investment? It's sometimes the ugliest, nasty, run-down eyesore that no one else wants to even look at. Investing can be emotional. When everyone's excited, you should worry. If everyone is worried, you should be looking for the opportunity. Don't listen to the false information which allows others to profit from your fear. You create opportunities to prosper from their greed!

This phenomenon doesn't only happen with tangible items. It also occurs in many of our relationships. We gravitate to things or people that cost us the most yet provide little value other than a temporary, emotional high. We throw away relationships that we have a vested interest in and provides us with valuable nutrition. The day to day trials of life push us back into our comfort zones and keep us in our status quo thinking. The Possibility Law will keep us focused and remind us what's available to you individually is also available for the collective whole.

O.G. Code - Hope Dealers

Throughout this book, I've emphasized the difference between our old mindset and living a new life with a new mindset. To those of you who once lived on the "block," we are now buying it. The game has changed and we have a new product. This product needs to flood our communities like crack cocaine did in the 1980's. It is imperative that we don't let old mindsets trip us up at this point. As we embrace new possibilities remember this Law with these eight commandments:

- Choose the impossible. If it were easy everybody would do it. O.G., change your community one life at a time.
- Don't sleep on your imagination. Learn to dream again. If you can't see it before you see it then you'll never see it.
- Stop trying to get "Higher." None of the artificial stimulants of today (fame, fortune, notoriety) will get you there. Appreciate what has worked all along; character, integrity, respect. It's these common enhancements that will take you to queen and kingship.
- Embrace your resourcefulness. If you focus on what you don't have, you will always have lack. If you focus on what you have, there is opportunity.
- Organize your community. We masterfully play the corporate

game every day because we want the promotion. Your community needs, and will appreciate, you more.

- Teach your community. There are some who are counting on your ignorance. Ignorant people are easier to control. There is no learning without teachers.

- Love your community. Love is an action word. Our community's love language is service. What does your love look like?

Conclusion

Hopefully, after reading The Possibility Law, you can believe not only for others, and their success, but for your own success and the success of your community. The key is to change what you focus on and take responsibility for the direction we're traveling in life.

The Possibility Law keeps us focused forward and stops us from looking back. Looking back can prove fatal. The biblical story of Lot's wife turning into a pillar of salt suggests the same. The problem with looking back is that it stops us from being in the present. It also prevents us from even showing up in the future. Many sweepstakes prize money, tax refunds, and other monetary sums go unclaimed yearly because nobody showed up to claim what was theirs. As we will see in the next chapter, being present, just showing up, is crucial. Mark your calendar, be on time and don't hesitate. We have a date with Destiny and she doesn't like to be kept waiting.

Success doesn't come to you...You go to it.

– *Marva Collins*

Chapter XII - Date with Destiny
The Presence Law
Take your seat at the table

If you're not at the table then you're on the menu. Make sure your agenda is spelled out and priced correctly.

Show Up!

When I was in college, and even in high school, there was always that class where the teacher put more emphasis on class participation than on written work and assignments. Basically, if you showed up for the course, you were guaranteed a passing grade. Understanding this, it seems everyone would show up to class. There was always, for whatever reason, the one or two students who didn't show up. How many times have you not shown up because you did not believe you had the skill or ability to be in the room?

I heard someone say if you're not at the "table," you are on the "menu." We also know if we are the smartest person in the room, we are in the wrong place. We know in life there will be assignments we must complete, and there will be work that needs to be turned in, but how many times have we forfeited opportunity because we did not show up? Why don't we show up? Insecurity? Not feeling worthy? Fear? It may be all the above. The Presence Law addresses your "imposter syndrome."

For many years, I went through life feeling like I wasn't worthy of the best that life had to offer me. This continued beyond having signs of moderate success. The credentials, a job, and family; I had it all. When I plateaued, I plateaued hard. In fact, the area of my plateau seemed so vast I couldn't tell that I was on a mountain nor could I not see how far I had ascended. I later realized it was this lack of belief in myself that caused me to turn a blind eye toward my destiny and how far I had come. It took me 12 years to get my first four-year degree (I was on the three for one plan. For every year I should have been there, I gave them three).

Many people who are successful take the scenic route. It takes longer than we anticipate, and unfortunately, we forget to celebrate the accomplishment. So, you can have everything it takes to succeed and lack the confidence to walk through the door. The O.G. is confident because in most cases you will do the total opposite of the status quo. If you have what it takes, all you need is to show up. When you do finally show up, don't be reluctant to shine and shine brightly. The Presence Law allows us to shine bright, like diamonds. Marianne Williamson said it best:

"Our deepest fear is not that we are inadequate. Our deepest fear is that we are powerful beyond measure. It is our light, not our darkness that most frightens us. We ask ourselves, who am I to be brilliant, gorgeous, talented, and fabulous? Actually, who are you not to be? You are a child of God. Your playing small does not serve the world. There is nothing enlightened about shrinking so that other people will not feel insecure around you. We are all meant to shine, as children do. We were born to make manifest the glory of God that is within us. It is not just in some of us; it is in everyone, and as we let our own light shine, we unconsciously give others permission to do the same. As we are liberated from our own fear, our presence automatically liberates others."

Yes, O.G., you are something to see. Get used to everyone looking at you because you are that Black Swan. Don't shy away from your greatness.

211

All Eyes on Me

Throughout my college years 99 percent of the time, I was the only black man in the classroom. I was a nontraditional student. Toward my later years in college, most of the time, I was the oldest student in the class. As an older student, you feel foolish when you don't know the answer. It's like you've had a three, five, ten-year head start on your peers you're sitting next to, and yet in this domain, you are no better off. Fast forward to my professional career, and I find myself in a similar predicament only this time it's a boardroom and not a classroom. Now, as a rookie, you feel that everyone knows more than what you know. Many times, I lacked the confidence to make meaningful contributions. I was a great support player, but I didn't shine.

You are qualified. You have the credentials and you have the experience. You even have unique qualifications learned outside of your profession. What causes your feelings to be at odds with reality? It's called imposter syndrome. No one wants to be a fake O.G. This is where the tales that are told are more fabulous than the work that is put in. You will hear the saying, "fake it until you make it," but pretending takes you only so far. This is not a case of you being a fake O.G. You have put in the work and you did what it takes to succeed.

We talked a little bit in chapter five about our mindset playing tricks on us. Imposter syndrome is a mindset that does not allow us to see how great we are. This mindset plagues our community because we have many capable individuals who can lead, but are lacking an understanding of The Presence Law. We are missing from the table, and if we are present, we don't speak loud enough. The table can be the boardroom table, city council table, state and even national government tables.

I heard a preacher ask a question once in his sermon. He said, "If you are put on trial for being a Christian, is there enough evidence to convict you?" There is a mountain of evidence to convict you of being a person of great character, integrity, and knowledge of the task at hand.

"Objection!" you say, "it's all circumstantial."
You then proceed to present an argument pointing out and dissecting any and every flaw in the case for your greatness. Imposter syndrome has struck again. Imposter syndrome can keep you from getting started because you don't think you're worthy. It also can stop you from finishing what you started because you have not "perfected" it yet. Here are four steps to help you with imposter syndrome.

1. Develop a sense of urgency.

Movement is better than stagnation. Don't allow your momentum to slow and understand time is not on your side.

2. Try and pinpoint where this feeling comes from.

There may be an unresolved issue that needs to be addressed.

3. Talk to someone.

Talking will allow you to see objectively what this is doing to your progress and adds some accountability.

4. Stop trying to be perfect.

Set strict deadlines for yourself and move on.

I don't know who said practice makes perfect, but it is not a correct statement. It will only make an improvement. If we try hard enough it can always become better. You will never be perfect so don't let that hinder you from starting.

Let imperfection work for you

One of my first jobs was for a commercial bakery in my hometown. We were a high-volume bread and bun producer. Quality control over the product ensured there was a balance between putting out a great product and the speed in which we could do it. We would run bread or bun production at various speeds throughout the production cycle depending upon the demand. The slower we would run our machinery the more "perfect" each loaf, bun, breadstick, or whatever it was we were making at the time would drop into the pan. The result was a great looking product. The profitability of the plant depended upon quality and speed. There were times when we really had the place cranking. The product still looked good, but as not as good as on a slower day. If we were within specific tolerances, there was no such thing as "ugly" bread.

I would like to challenge you when imposter syndrome, perfectionism, or over-analysis stops you from going forward, understand that time is money. You are either making "ugly" bread or no bread. Set your boundaries, but not so tight that nothing can make it through. Perfect starvation is what you'll end up with and it does not look good on you. Remember, there's no such thing as "ugly" bread.

Will the real O.G. please stand up? Your community needs to eat. Now is not the time to shy away, slow down, or lose focus. The Presence Law is backed with confidence. It's not false confidence but supported by the undeniable fact that it's your time. It's your time O.G.!

All the work we did in Parts I and II allows you to step on the scene with boldness. It allows you to keep your head when everyone around you is losing theirs. It will enable you to know, go, and grow forward when the world around you becomes complacent and satisfied with little or nothing. You have already been through the fire. Who's going to stop you? If you show up consistently, the results will take care of themselves. Trust the process. "Done" is better than "perfect!" The momentum built from finishing far outweighs the heaviness of stagnation. None of us are perfect even though sometimes we think we are. But this can't stop you from showing up. Practice being a failure.

The only person who never fails is a person who never attempts anything. Anytime there is the slightest possibility of you growing and succeeding, go for it. It's a numbers game. When enough of us understand this, and enough of us show up, change will take place. Become familiar with the planning commission. Show up at your children's school. Show up at the city council and attend a meeting. Visit your school board meetings; the police station and the courthouse. Show up anywhere you are not expected to be. It's the adhering to other's expectations of you that keeps the status quo. The O.G. – Obtaining Greatness mindset is anything but status quo.

Blind Dates

To say there is a lack of trust in our community would be an understatement (We will explore this a little deeper in chapter 14.). Is it difficult to believe that most folks are good people when your experience has shown you otherwise? Even though our experiences with some people outside of our communities have been negative, exploitive, and condemning, this is not a time to shrink. If you get the short end of the stick consistently then your reality is different from someone who has experienced the opposite of the transaction. Understand this and develop a sense of empathy when you engage people who think differently than you. This is not to give someone a pass on behaving ignorantly, but keeps you from showing up expecting one thing and being disappointed when you receive another. The guy you are pointing your finger at, guess what, he's not going to change. When you show up, you don't have to marry the situation, just explore it. Very little will change overnight, and the things that do, won't last very long if you were not involved in facilitating.

No area is perfect, but some communities will practice focusing on the good instead of the bad. It's easy to blame the news organizations and the "system" but check the average Facebook account and watch the "news" that is proudly displayed across our social media timelines. We can blame the algorithms and such, but more than likely someone had to press "share."

I'm not here to indict but to challenge you to embrace you inner O.G. despite of what society looks like. If we wait for perfect conditions we will wait forever. What are some of the negatives happening in your environment? You know you must act in spite of them. Write them down. Don't allow foolishness to stop progress.

Recognize and celebrate when you show up successfully and accomplish your goal, regardless of the negatives. Now, can you show up and be embarrassed? Can you show up and flop? Or, can you show up and be harshly criticized by your community, or worse? These are possibilities but which is better? To show up and fail or not show up and regret that you never tried? You have a gift that is needed by our community. It may not be accepted at first. You must build trust and rapport. Those who you are trying to help don't want your help if it does not feel genuine.

Body Language

"Presence," as defined by Amy Cuddy in her book "Presence: Bringing Your Boldest Self to Your Biggest," is the state of being attuned to, and being able to comfortably express our true thoughts, feelings, values, and potential. We know what we want to say. We know how we feel, but so often we don't know how to express it orally. Your spoken communication is only half the battle. Non-verbal cues are manifested in the way we carry ourselves physically. Sometimes, this can speak louder than we can orally. What is the "body" saying?

Our community has lacked a unified message or response. Do we need an agenda? This is a topic outside the realm of this book, but I had to address it briefly. A unified message is like the firm handshake while looking a man in his eye. Contrarily, guess what a limp hand extended while you sheepishly look away will get you? Someone could take advantage of you and perceive this as weakness. I can hear some of you saying that looking a man in the eye is disrespectful in some cultures. You missed the point. I'm sure if you were at my house or I at yours, different rules may apply. Sometimes we show up demanding our personal rules apply to a situation. This only works if you have the power to back it up. Always respect protocol for sake of the long game.

How do you get a body as large and diverse as the black community to speak the same language? That's a great question! Unfortunately, I don't have an answer. But, we've played "go along to get along" for decades in corporate America. How much more should we be willing to give for each other, the community and our future? If you're a true O.G., serving your community should be in your blood. Remember everybody eats, and it is your responsibility to take the lessons from Parts I and II of this book to heart. Most can't. I'm speaking to the few who can. If there are figureheads in your community who are not O.G.'s, don't support them. If you have politicians in your state and the local electorate who are not O.G.'s, don't re-elect them.

Divide and conquer is an ancient strategy and you must recognize when it's being played. There is power in unity. If it looks like you can accomplish your individual agenda if you break from the group, this is almost always a divide and conquer play. The O.G. – Obtaining Greatness mindset is the opposite of selfishness. There is no such thing as a selfish O.G. Let's have the confidence to show up in solidarity, and not be persuaded by trinkets of capitalism. This can happen when you take control of your destiny and live independently of structures put in place to keep the status quo. I should remind you everyone is not an O.G. You grow to a point where you've seen some things in life and the Okie Doke doesn't work anymore. You have history and context, perspective. You will know the fake when you see it.

Through the fire

We've been to hell and back again. And death cannot have the final word. - *Ossie Davis*

I want to pose a question. Do you think the worst is over? There are only two ways to answer this question. If you answer yes, you are acknowledging the progress that has been made and a present state which is far more desirable than the former. You are speaking with the understanding that while conditions may not be optimal, they are better than what they were before. What if you don't believe the worst is over? Then your answer is no and you are probably braced for the struggle ahead. Either way, get ready to put in work. Either way, we all have been through something. My wise uncle would always tell me whenever I complained to him, "If you're going through, be sure to keep on going."

Everyone has a different perception and a different perspective of our community. No one should disagree that there is still work to be done. Asking questions about the past should never allow you to lose sight of your future. What are you doing today to obtain a brighter future? Remember, don't get stuck looking back. Onward! If you are down by a touchdown or field goal, now is not the time to criticize plays. We do this as a community. Whether we win or lose this battle, the next step is always to grow, get better, and come back stronger.

Birthday Presence

Service is a gift and also the price for admission. Instead of being divided where we are pushed to the right or to the left, understand that O.G.'s come in all shapes sizes and colors. The best play to call in these circumstances would be to run directly up the middle. There are other people out there who are blocking and tackling for you. You must recognize there is a hole for you to run through. That hole is only open when someone shows up to run through it. Don't cry about the defense because that's part of the game. If you don't show up that hole won't be open for very long.

An O.G. seizes the moment and takes advantage of every opportunity. It is a very competitive world. It's not a world where you can shrink and expect someone to hand something to you. It is a world you have been equipped to compete in as you show up for practice and show up for the games, win or lose.

In life, you have options. If you are advancing on the field of life, and the situation changes, quickly adjust. For example, if an election doesn't go your way, or the economy heads south, don't act like a deer in the headlights. Read the play! If the economy is at an all-time high, and the stock market is roaring understand what comes next.

Learn to adjust accordingly. For most of us this is a new game. We are used to playing defense, and when it comes to offense, all we know is man-to-man. If our community is to be on one accord, we must understand more positions than just our own. We must be more strategic and be prepared to learn more than one play. O.G. you are a winner from a community of winners. The way you win politically, economically, and socially is by showing up. If possible, don't show up empty handed. Bring a gift. This is step one and you can't skip it. There is no winning, and there should be no celebration, if you're not even at the table.

O.G. Code - Table Manners

Politics is a part of life. You need to learn how to play the game to better your community. There is strength in numbers, but you should be patient to build a coalition and consensus around issues. Don't be afraid of the status quo but challenge it! When the status quo pushes, politely push back.

- You can make decisions for your community. You will not be liked by everyone and this is not an indication of your leadership ability.
- Show up in your home with your wife and kids. In your extended family effect change and provide encouragement. An O.G.'s presence is felt and will set the temperature instead of just measuring it.
- Your time to lead is inevitable and was appointed when you

asked "Why" early on in your life. Your "Why," or your reason for being here will always impact other people. God works through people. An O.G. is a vessel. Take your assignment seriously.

- Understand what and where decisions are made that affect your community and sign up to volunteer. This includes all governing bodies both appointed and elected. If you are not an appointed or elected official then be sure you're in the audience.

- Politics are a part of life, just like capitalism. Learn the rules of the game and play to win. We like to play football and basketball. Change your mindset, change your life.

- You have been battle tested in various trials and difficulties of life. The learned self-preservation will provide you with your next step whenever you're faced with a challenge you don't readily know how to handle.

- People can think they're greater than they really are, but an O.G. actually is greater than he or she thinks of himself or herself. You are not an imposter!

Conclusion

Sometimes it's intimidating to exercise our authority in venues we are not use to. Status quo would say go with the flow and just stay out of those places. This mentality must be challenged. Do you remember a time in life when you didn't have a clue how you were going to make it? At that moment, it was clear to you all sources had been exhausted and there was no way. Yet, here you are. I'm sure there was more than one occasion like this. What do you think happens when you repeatedly make it out of tight situations? These situations can be financial or otherwise. Something happens over time that you may not be aware of. Let's explore this sixth sense O.G. - Obtaining Greatness trait that allows us to have "instant recall" when facing tough situations.

Self-esteem means knowing you are the dream.

– Oprah Winfrey

Chapter XIII - Hustle Memory
The Preparation Law
Your life created you for prosperity

Survival is built into your physiological make-up. Thriving is part of your spiritual DNA. Accepting this mentally is the connection.

(Wall) Street Player

Were you one of those kids who played in the street without regard to the perils of traffic? At one time, it amazed me the nerve of some children. I remember the first time I allowed my daughter to cross the street by herself at a traffic stop. She may have been around eight years old, and although we had managed traffic many times together, a father doesn't want to take any risk with his children. But what would happen if I didn't allow her to cross the street until she'd gone away to college and had no other choice? She would not have been adequately prepared for what lay ahead. No risk, no reward.

We've all been risk takers in varying degrees all our lives. Today, you hear terms like "free-range" parenting versus "helicopter" parenting. Parents want their children to be safe and at the same time, have some "street" sense. As parents, we can easily cross the line by sheltering our children to the point they can't operate without us. We do them a disservice unintentionally. The Preparation Law gives you an unnoticed advantage. It's like an anti-virus software that's been running in the background. You can say its artificial intelligence running simulations of every past experience to deliver a desired outcome. For my faith filled friends Jeremiah 29:11, "For I know the thoughts that I think toward you, saith the LORD, thoughts of peace, and not of evil, to give you an expected end."

If you ever talked to anyone who grew up during the Great Depression, or even more recently the great recession, they are probably more frugal than the average American. Depression-era Americans took fewer risks with their money. These folks had the "cash under the mattress" mindset. All our risk experiences in life prepare us and mold us for the chances we are willing to, or not willing to, take today.

Are you an ultra-conservative investor? Or, are you more of an aggressive investor? Like the "helicopter" parent, it's possible you may be doing more harm than good. If your conservative nature allows you to depend only on the company you work for, and you equate this with safety, this can be a serious problem unless you own the company.

In many communities ownership seems, and I emphasize the word "seems," riskier then renting. By renting I mean trading your hours for dollars or any transaction that doesn't involve equity. In our community, you will see some of the most talented individuals with million dollar gifts. Prosperity is calling your name, but you must learn the sound of her voice. That sound can be music to your ears.

A little bit of night music

When I was a kid I slept with the radio playing. Those slow jams rocked me to sleep and comforted me throughout my childhood. On Saturday mornings, while simultaneously cleaning the house and watching cartoons, my mom and my uncle would jam to the "oldies but goodies" on the radio. I sang in my elementary school choir under the direction of my sixth-grade teacher, Mrs. D.V. Dixon. I grew up in the hip-hop era. My friends and I would recite rhymes into the late hours of the night. I even became a pretty decent writer of poetry, spoken word and, now, books.

When my first child was born, I would put her to bed at night with Mozart playing in the background. I did this for each of my children although it seems that my son was the only one that would become musically inclined. Among his many musical talents he is an incredible saxophone player. So, how does all this wisdom, expertise, knowledge, foresight, insight, love of learning and preparation equip us as individuals separately, and as a community?

The Preparation Law works when you begin to operate in your gift and profit from it. The key words here are "you" and "profit." In Part II of this book, we talked about owning the means of production. Music is a perfect example. We know historically, artists made a lot less money than the music companies, managers or anyone claiming to have the artist's best interest. I think the late artist Prince said it best, "If you don't own your masters, your masters own you." Monetize your gift, talents, and intellect. In the past, you reaped a minimal benefit for you, your family and community. Massive riches were garnered by second and third parties. Today, you own your "masters." The playing field has been laid and the table set to allow you to reap the rewards of your labor. Those of you not of the O.G. mindset like to point out the fact that the playing field is not level. A true O.G. will win anyway.

Immigrants come to America every day with eager amazement of the opportunity waiting for them. Then, they exploit the rules of capitalism ravenously. They devour opportunity like it was morsels of food and they were dying of starvation. As an O.G., you've matched that same level of commitment to winning this game, and at this stage, it doesn't matter. You can't wait until the field is perfectly level to win. The earlier you learn this, the sooner it's embedded in your psyche and in the mind of your children; the sooner you win.

Music is one example of an industry where the few controlled the talented many. We enlist in this army believing it's the only way. Your nine to five job has prepared you to go A.W.o.L. This is the acronym that I use for "Alternative Wealth or Labor." In this capitalist society "labor," from a business perspective, is an expense. It's a means to an end, and if we can do more with less labor, that is considered a good thing. This is a good thing because now we have more profit and where does this profit go? It goes to the owners, or shareholders, and increases for shareholders, is another way of saying wealth creation. Depending on which side of this equation you spend most of your time, you receive equity, or you earn a wage or salary. The good news is you can choose which side of this equation you spend most of your time. Owning your "masters" is a decision that you must make up front. Then, you can plan and maneuver accordingly. When you change your mindset, you understand there is another way.

Letting the Master own you

God works through people. People, meaning you and me. When you avail yourself to God, He will put a song in your heart in the midnight hour. Weeping may endure for a night, but joy comes in the morning. When you least expect it all those years of work you put in will manifest itself in that "O.G. Thing." Whether it is in that song, that business idea or even a position within a great organization which will allow you to do something significant and meaningful for your community.

If you've ever found yourself where it seemed as if life had taken everything, and you had no place to turn, that was the Preparation Law in action. An O.G. knows where his help comes from. If you could make it through that, whatever "that" was, you'll make it through anything. This law gives you the confidence to do something different and not fear failure.

A love of your own

The average black man has been through many challenges in his life. Because of The Preparation Law you are more capable than you believe. You might not feel like you're ready to be the Chief Executive Officer of your own corporation, but you do just as much work for the CEO of someone else's corporation. Isn't it funny, how 80-hour work weeks for someone else, for someone else's children or for someone else's legacy is entirely doable? As an at-will employee! So, you think you're not prepared?

No, you won't start at the top. It will be a lot of hard work and you may even fail. Give God glory by exercising the gifts and talents that he has put inside of you. Too many of us die with unexecuted plans, blueprints and architectural drawings of the life we wish we had. You are already prepared and a construction crew waits for your command. Most of us have our foundation laid already, but fear stops us from framing a positive perception of ourselves.

Will you take the leap and allow God to grow your wings on the way down? God has never let me hit rock bottom. Those who I have seen hit rock bottom received just what they needed to rebuild their lives and soar today. I've also seen people on top of the world today and gone from this world tomorrow. I don't pretend to understand why that is or try and make sense out of the tragedies of life. With the limited understanding I have, that's enough for me to say go for it! Tomorrow's not promised to you. As motivational speaker Les Brown says, "You can't get out of life alive!"

Alternative Wealth or Labor

I want to take time to clarify the fact that not everyone will own a physical "brick and mortar" company. Also, it's okay to work for someone else; only if you CHOOSE to. I put emphasis on the word choose. Understand few people become wealthy depending on a nine to five paycheck. If you want the big bucks working for someone else, that nine to five becomes a seven to seven with work on evenings and weekends. At some point, the law of diminishing returns kicks in. If you're not careful, you will turn that six-figure salary into a minimum wage job. I may be exaggerating, but only a little bit.

Time is your most valuable resource. You must maximize and protect it. You might ask, "What if I love my job?" I would never encourage anyone to quit their job, especially if you love it. If you're not yet of the O.G. mindset, you will find yourself in an even worse position if you do. O.G. - Obtaining Greatness mindset is for employees too! This excellence is a way of life. A company knows when an O.G. works for it. It shows in the quality of your work. A simple way to become wealthy while keeping your job is to accumulate appreciating assets.

My uncle Jim worked over 30 years for General Motors (GM). He and his wife, my aunt Ethel, both worked for GM. He poured iron and she worked in the cafeteria. Their wealth was made through their passive income portfolio.

We can do this today as well, but we also have the internet. This provides almost limitless income possibilities. When I was a kid, I watched a ton of television. Way more than what I now consider healthy. Today, it's not T.V., but the internet. It's the same players with different technologies. The masses continue to consume while a few savvy business people produce content to keep us "entertained." This is important on several levels, but I'll stick with alternative wealth for now. When you were a kid did you think T.V. was free? I know I did. If you didn't have cable those three to five channels still did the trick. What I did not realize was the value of my attention to advertisers. Your eyeballs are for sale and so is your information. The O.G. is very aware and has a keen sense of what's going on around him. Get in on this action.

Buyers and sellers

"Today I begin a new life for I am the master of my abilities and today is going to be a great and beautiful day..."

This line comes from the iconic scene of one of my favorite movies "Baby Boy," written, produced and directed by the late John Singleton. It's a coming of age tale of a young man growing up in the inner city. Listen as the main character Jody, played by actor Tyrese Gibson, explains to his friend Pea how the game goes.

"Pea you a buyer or a seller?"
"Huh?"
"How many millionaires you got on? I count at least three."
"Man, what the fuck are you talking about?"
"Pea! Look around man! You see what I see? I see money! Brother over there selling T-shirts. Brother selling pies getting paper. Cake Man over there. Everybody moving and making money while we're standing still being broke! I figured all this shit out man. All of this, this whole world moves forward through transactions. Commerce Nigga! The exchange of goods and services. All the real ballers and successful folks are sellers, and all the broke ass people playing catch-up are buyers. I ain't going out like that Pea. I'm going to be a seller. I'm going to get my own business and change the game."

What Jody was speaking of is the O.G. – Obtaining Greatness mindset. Twenty years later the game is still the same. You're prepared for this because you've seen it before. It's the same opportunity, just chose your vehicle; real estate, technology, the financial markets. Don't miss out on the opportunity before you.

Be greedy when others are fearful and fearful when others are greedy. - *Warren Buffet*

The O.G. mindset lets you take a step back and see what's really going on. When you fully understand, and comprehend, how capitalism works, a lot of us will choose to leave or go A.W.o.L to the corporate machine. There are some great companies out there. Yours can be one of them. The sooner you recognize that you have options, the sooner we get to have our own.

Corporate Prayer

After you have obtained your opportunity, it is time to focus on creating opportunities for others. People who only seek a "job" rarely, or never, grow to be job creators. Some poor people don't want to be rich. Some people can't think beyond their needs. They don't ask, "How can I meet the needs of others?" Watch the O.G. mindset. If you help enough people get what they need, then your needs will be easily met (This includes being the very BEST employee if you do work for someone else). An O.G. believes that everyone eats.

I get excited if I see my brother doing well. It encourages me to play my position to the best of my ability. Life has prepared you for this moment to lead. In your household, I'm sure you put the needs of your spouse, children, aging parents, and others before your own. If you love, you can lead. You may say, "I'm tired, at my wit's end and plain worn out." I like the wisdom Moses received in the book of Exodus from his father in law Jethro. Jethro told Moses to get help and delegate some responsibilities. If he didn't, Moses would not have lasted. Instead of praying only for the jobs, pray for the job creators, then create!

I'm not naive to anyone who has caught a bad break in life. If you happen to be between opportunities, everyone can serve. If you feel there's no other choice but a J.O.B. you can rub elbows with the "movers and shakers" by volunteering. You have time; change your mindset. We all get the same 24 hours, and should you ever find yourself without opportunity or employment, serve your community even more. One hour in the right place at the right time can be worth 100 job applications. As we move from "corporate" to "cooperate" something almost magical begins to happen. The conversation shifts from "I need" to "I can help." What do you bring to the table? How does your life experience prepare you for meeting the needs of your community or the company?

Although I sometimes sound anti-corporation, I am not. We just need to focus on the right side of the accounting equation, Assets - Liabilities = Owners Equity. Don't get stuck in the middle; no assets and no equity with a lot of liabilities. You may not even want to be someone else's liability or employee (you know that's what they call employees). While there are some great corporate citizens, we can use a few more corporations led by people operating with the O.G. - Obtaining Greatness mindset.

My prayer is that all the lessons learned from the obstacles we have overcome individually will lead to our collective "better self"; our better social, economic and political selves. If you made it this far then making money in America will be a piece of cake. Redirect your focus and energy then watch how success becomes second nature. You are used to overcoming and succeeding.

Because I Love You

God so loved the world that He gave his only begotten Son that whoever believed in him would not perish but have everlasting life - *John 3:16*

This book is birthed out of my love for my community. As I stated before, these principles are not new and have stood the test of time. They are probably written in a way you have never heard them but nothing new. I see you grinding every day. Your children see you, too. They will do what you do, but be careful before you pat yourself on the back. The grind can wear you out prematurely if you're not careful, and your children. More money plus more spending is not sustainable long-term. Grow your margins back to a healthy place where you don't need two incomes, or paycheck to paycheck living.

Grow to a place where it's not only about the grind but about becoming your best self. You might not believe in living this way but give it a try. It won't kill you and I promise life will be more fulfilling. Don't forget your "Why" while you grind. If you do, you will face the law of diminishing returns. Every additional achievement will start to bring in less and less fulfillment. Each additional dollar will be the same.

Don't let the grind turn into a "chasing Jason" scenario and you hurt the ones you love. You will never get that same "high." Love is what prepared you. It's what brings you home at night after a day in the field. Someone loved you through those tough times and He (our Creator) will love you into abundance!

On too many occasions we misunderstand our love because of the season of life that we're in. Life happens to all of us and that "O.G. thing" can succumb to temporary blindness. When we can't

233

see it, love looks like it's evading us and purposely staying out of our reach. As life continues, and we seem like we're walking blind, the other senses are heightened. Hence, faith is strengthened. Success will not evade you. It's just a matter of knowing what season you are in and how to love through it.

Love and Marriage

Have you ever seen a married couple who argued and nagged each other all the time? The sarcasm and cynicism are unreal and the monotony of the relationship, from the outside looking in, would bore anyone to death. Compared to your temporary connections, they've been together forever. You see these folks and Al and Peggy Bundy come to mind. Every night when they go to bed they know they have lived to fight another day.

In the beginning, the "hustle" doesn't look like you imagined but this is the preparation process. Too many times we attempt to short-cut the process only to extend our holding pattern and risk running out of fuel. Understand most of the time, the grind is boring. Those of us who are visually stimulated must take extra precautions to keep from taking two steps forward and three back. Stay focused!

I've referenced the "long game" throughout this book because too many times we succumb to the need for instant gratification. Big Ma was married to Granddad for 60 years and had 10 times the problems newlyweds face today. It was different times but the same problems. They were problem solvers. Problem solvers have longevity.

Love and Hip Hop

There is a difference between the O.G. – Obtaining Greatness mindset "hustler" and a "hollywood hustler" Hollywood wants to be seen hustling. It is part of his make-up and sometimes he can't sit still. The O.G. mindset will cause you to escape the spotlight and avoid the drama that comes along with "shining." Classic Hip-Hop has always been about the "come up." "Shining" often has a lot to do with your self-esteem. Suppose, for a second, what would happen if our community lost its desire to "shine?" Hip-Hop would again have a message, the buyer/seller equation would flip on its head and wealth would transfer. This is a very simplistic hypothetical and I by no means want to propose change without any action steps. I do believe when you love people, starting with yourself, there's less room for the wretchedness of life.

If you depend less on your natural eyes certain people, behaviors, and habits won't have a place in your life for very long. Love is an action word and I don't believe true love causes us to be worse off. In this day of texting and social media, rarely do we just listen to the sound of a person's voice. We miss what's being said, but what's not being said becomes the norm. The defining silence that represents the fullness of our current relationships with each other overtakes the conscious messages we used to share. Life is more than the "hustle."

Love and Basketball

The Preparation Law equipped you with the fundamentals you need for today. This has been going on your whole life. When no one was looking, you ran, dribbled, shot, scraped a knee, twisted an ankle, practiced and traveled. You sacrificed time and money. What we face in our community today is not more difficult than challenges we have met in the past. What we've overcome in the past. It's no fun to watch a basketball game with someone who doesn't enjoy basketball.

I talked before about being "equally yoked," or partnering with someone with a similar level of preparation. Embrace diversity and learn from the tastes and cultures of others. There must be a shared vision regardless of who is leading. Can you buy into this vision?

We will need defense and offense to win this game, specifically, more offense. Finding someone you can live with is not that hard. It's the one you can't live without that will make all the difference. Get that person on your team. Teamwork makes the dream work.

Love and Happiness

In my life's journey, and my attempts to grow professionally and financially, I have spent too much time focusing on things rather than on the people I said I loved. Love is an action word and it creates happy memories. Or, it makes hard situations easier to bare. It's being present, listening and not always talking. My vision is to make my wife and children happy. This other stuff means nothing if I can't do that. I know what you're thinking, "You can't make another person happy." Yes, but that won't stop me from trying and giving my all. I can create the atmosphere.

It is imperative that we forever seek ways to do something instead of listing all the reasons why we cannot. That is the O.G. – Obtaining Greatness mindset. It provides a soundtrack for a life full of love and happiness. When you master this, you can put a smile on someone's face as soon as they hear your vocals.

When the beat and cadence of your leadership invite the cords that bind the cultural composition together then we will hear, see and feel love like the happiest memories of our childhood. It will move you in a way like nothing else can and put you in a prosperous state of mind. This is your song written in the key of life that elevates all your senses no matter what you can see physically. This O.G. life was composed with you in mind.

Major Keys

There are keys we need to help keep the Preparation Law operating in our favor.

Key 1 - Start where you are and budget what you have now.

This includes time, money and other resources. You'll be surprised how wealth creation becomes second nature and generational with this one habit.

Key 2 - Stay objective.

It's easy to let your emotions get the best of you and give you a false sense of accomplishment or failure. All of those "mistakes" you thought you made in the past were actually practice for today. If you made it then you'll make it now.

Key 3 - Learn from other people's success.

You will fall short playing not to lose. We are just playing defense at this point. With offense we begin to model success and more success will follow. Don't allow your pride to stop you from modeling a successful person God has allowed into your life (He works through people).

Key 4 - Be aggressive in your growth.

Now that you are aware of the challenges you beat in the past, you can't afford to become passive. Your practice should be harder than the game. Actively look for ways to win and don't take "no" for an answer. When it comes to growth, go hard or go home.

Enhance the part of you that has learned how to find a way or to make one. Your faith is like a GPS system and it has delivered you through the trials and tribulations of life's journey. How much sense would it make to get to this stage of the mission and to turn off your GPS? Even if you know what your destination looks like, it is great to hear that confirmation, "You have arrived at your destination." If we have come this far by Faith, it would be foolish to think God would place the keys in the hands of your enemy for the last leg of this journey. The keys are in your hands. Exercise your Faith and know you are prepared.

Scientific Method, Man

I always believed Faith and science went hand in hand. This is not an either-or question, but a yes and yes. So, while you're "holding to God's unchanging hand," check your cash consciousness.

Observation - <u>Cash</u> is coveted.

O.G. - Obtaining Greatness mindset - Accumulate positive cash flow generating assets. What I have observed in my career advising high net worth individuals is that 90 percent of them accumulated their wealth outside of nine to five employment. They had a rule for their cash.

Question - What are the <u>rules</u> for cash?

O.G. - Obtaining Greatness mindset - Cash should always work for you. Your dollars should be working for you while you are sleeping. Keep them "employed" and when one task ends another task, or investment, begins.

Hypothesis - Money isn't <u>everything</u>.

O.G. - Obtaining Greatness mindset - This is never an excuse to be broke. While this premise may have some truth to it, you can't allow it to justify your sub-par financial position. If you just state the obvious you will miss out on a higher reality. Money is significant in our lives.

Experiment - Hang <u>around</u> people with more money than you.

O.G. - Obtaining Greatness mindset - Your mastermind means everything. You reflect the people you hang around the most. Their

238

ideas, their values and their rules on wealth will rub off on you. Also, note that almost all the time they will rub off on you before you rub off on them. So, keep your circle tight and right.

Conclusion - No one can stop <u>me</u> from designing my financial destiny.

O.G. - Obtaining Greatness mindset - We do it for the culture. If cash is the only thing you're looking for, you have missed the point. The O.G. mindset always looks at the bigger picture. The goal is to instill these laws into your DNA so it stays with your children and your children's children.

O.G. Code - The 'G'nome

Our community is a moving, breathing, living organism made up of a rich, flavorful culture. "Hustle" is in the DNA of our culture. The strength and greatness of our ancestors is an inheritance which can't be denied. Understand the season you are in and the opportunities presented all around you. This has prepared us for a jubilee that will shift our economic condition because our collective mindset has made a shift. Life is not a zero-sum game. There is plenty for everyone. Adopt the following prep code in your community.

- Bank your sequence - To propagate the O.G. code in our community you must document your plan. Write it down!
- Clones - Copy successful offense. We have masterful defensive plays and nothing can destroy us. Work on your assault and work on mounting successful attacks.
- Market Metabolism - Our community diet must consist of ideas that speed up our metabolism in the marketplace. Take advantage of innovation and entrepreneurship. This leads to a

lean life of economic strength and burns the fat of dependency.

- Time Theory - The illusion of time will make you underestimate what you can accomplish in five years and overestimate what you can achieve today. Focus on one thing at a time. Complete your goal then move to the next one.
- Multiverse - Don't relate and identify with the difficulties of today without identifying with the greatness of our ancestors or the future greatness to come in your life. Remember the struggle of life ebbs and flows. Learn to compartmentalize, visit when necessary but don't park too long. Travel light and keep it moving.

Conclusion

Each of us have a seed within. This seed may be dormant but time has kept it alive. Yes, you are prepared, but preparation does not fortify you against an opponent attempting to disrupt your environment. Specific rules need to be in place to ensure longevity and continuity of this blessing. The next chapter will give you insights to safeguard the O.G. mindset, lifestyle and community.

Accept responsibility for your life.
Know that it is you who will get you
where you want to go, no one else.

— *Les Brown*

Chapter XIV - Safe House
The Protection Law
You must serve and protect

Love your community enough to protect your community. You will serve what you love. Check yourself or be checked.

Every breath you take

Wealth can be measured in time. How many months or years can your cash flow support you without eating into your principle? Financial freedom happens when your cash flow is sufficient to meet your lifestyle. Economic freedom allows you to breathe more comfortably by easing the stress of supporting you and your family and provides the peace of mind that comes with choice.

Peace of mind is a form of protection. Protection in the physical sense that you don't worry about anyone invading your person. You also don't worry about where your next meal will come from. I want to go a little deeper into discussing our physical protection. Let's consider it from the perspective of the O.G. – Obtaining Greatness mindset.

When you think of physical security the first thing that comes to mind is some sort of altercation. We think of police brutality, Black on black crime or terrorism. Now, on the surface, these atrocities are visible in our society. It is what makes the headlines on the 24-hour news cycle. These various conditions did not happen overnight and, again, to combat these issues we must look at our long game. Addressing police brutality directly is beyond the scope of this book.

An O.G. does not want to fight, physically. When you strategize to win a war, you understand there will be some battles you will have to sacrifice. A strategic thinker will choose which battles to forgo. In business, the term loss-leader is used to describe a product which is sold at a loss to attract additional consumers. Tax-loss harvesting is a tax strategy used to realize losses in one area of your investment portfolio to offset realized gains in other investments, minimizing your tax liability. What seems to be a loss to the untrained eye, is a broader perspective gain.

The tactics utilized to implement O.G. culture on an economic, social and individual level must always be deliberate, intentional, and with measured results. If those measures fail to yield, over time, a satisfactory outcome we will switch tactics. If we continue to preach, to march, to shout, to fight, and demand rights (without responsibilities), we do not understand the game that is being played. We do not know who the patsy is in that game. Ask yourself, "Is what I am about to say or do advancing my cause?" With word and deed be deliberate and intense toward your cause. The Protection Law puts your safety in your own hands.

Intensive Care

We are almost to the end of this book, but I must remind the reader that no one is coming to save you. Sometimes I believe we put too much faith in the government, church, our job or any other entity outside of ourselves. The reality is you are responsible. I am responsible.

The Protection Law is akin to the law of self-preservation. To be entirely free and protected we must police our own communities. Changing the "color" of our police forces is a daunting task without readily available recruits or policy that advocates for such. What's also daunting is adopting the mindset that we are responsible for what happens in our communities. We must care for our

243

communities on a level that surpasses what is normal in other communities. In many communities outside investment is viewed as a positive because you are adding to something that is already relatively stable. In many communities of color, however, we are on life support, and a lot of outside investment marginalizes current residents.

So, on one hand, we have our individual pride of ownership individually, and on the other hand, you must have a say collectively in the types of projects that get developed in our communities. Yes, the latter is a little bit trickier. It's not easy because most of those with the specific talents to build our communities eventually leave our communities.

The O.G. needs to come back, serve and protect. This is the type of "intensive" care that is needed today. When your goal is to stop the bleeding, the outward apparel is cut off with no regard to who the designer is. Likewise, if you do all the work in your community and your name does not show up in a footnote, that's okay. The goal is to stop the bleeding. Once your community is stabilized and you have designed a thriving community, quality will speak for itself. An O.G. knows he cannot do it alone. This mindset does not need credit or recognition for individual effort. Teamwork will make the dream work.

At this stage we cannot gamble on individual effort. The stakes are too high for any one person, or one group, or one anything to think they have all the answers. As we move further on the scale toward the individual and away from the collective our bet becomes more speculative.

The House Always Wins

In my old neighborhood, and many neighborhoods across this

country, law enforcement is hindered through what is called a "no snitch" policy. What this means is although crime has been committed, and there were witnesses to the crime, no one will come forward to say anything. We equate dodging the short-term pain and false sense of betrayal with doing something good for our community. Nothing could be further from the truth. Do you remember when you were growing up in your household with your siblings? Some of you were snitches, or some of you were always snitched on.

My kids are older now and have since moved on, but I remember when they were little they stayed true to their "story." No one snitched at our house. A severe problem arises when the home is threatened. I know you don't want to get in trouble, but if a fire starts you can't wait it out so you don't get in trouble. You can't save your brother or your sisters' butt from a spanking and threaten the well-being of everyone. If you continue with this behavior, and you are at an age where you should know better, you need to leave the house. Likewise, there are people in our community we love. They are our brothers and sisters. Sometimes they are our mothers and fathers and others whom we have grown up with all our lives. They are threatening to burn down the house, but like a mother's love, something keeps us from kicking them out.

I have zero tolerance for kids playing with matches in my house. We need to have zero tolerance for crime in our community. This is how we win, and if the house is not set up to win, you will soon be out of business. It's not that we don't love the perpetrators and understand to a certain extent their plight in society, but I will question the value of destroying our house to protect the culprit. Your home is where you find safety from the external forces that come against you. It's where you find shelter from the harsh elements that fall upon you.

None of us want to be over policed or profiled. We don't want overbearing laws within an unjust system. This is what we get when we operate according to this "street code." When you address this with old mindsets, you realize the "original gangsters" started and perpetuated this lifestyle in the first place. To "Obtain Greatness," you must serve, and encourage others to help, and know that no one's going to do it for you. If you have taken heed of the first two parts of this book, you have the tools available to you. This is worth emphasizing. We must reconstruct our communities. There is a degree of insulation from uncomfortable elements. It depends on how your house, or your community, is built.

Builders Code

Just like "street code" that is upheld, and to the detriment of our community, there is also a code you can embrace to ensure a base level of safety, accountability, and stability. The foundation has been set with the proper footings of personal and family responsibility. This provides a perpetual stake driven deep into our community that can now support the framework we need to protect future generations.

When I built my first home, one of the decisions presented in the planning process was would I frame with two-inch by four-inch (two by four's) or lumber studs that measured two-inch by six-inch (two by six's). At first glance, you would think two inches would not make much difference relative to the added cost. As my builder explained to me, those extra two inches gave me more room for insulating materials. I understood a little upfront cost would provide added comfort in the future. Living in extreme temperatures, this is very important. Keeping a home cool in 90-degree heat or warm in sub-zero winters depends a lot on your insulation. It's one of those building elements we can't take for granted and it's costly to let insulation become an afterthought. In many of our communities, the "block is hot," and new construction will need to upgrade how we frame and use modern building materials.

R-Value

My builder explained to me that R-value was the capacity of an insulating material to resist heat flow. The higher the R-value, the higher the insulating power. You may be wondering what does R-value have to do with the Protection Law, serving or having a "Safe House." In an O.G. community, R-value measures the level of "Respect" built into the various frameworks and institutions that make up our community. The greater the level of respect for these various institutions the less "heat" transfer. This is the start of maintaining a comfortable temperature no matter the climate or unpredictable weather patterns that come our way.

An O.G. mindset is focused on the long game and winning the war. It knows when it is expedient to give up a battle. Short-term thinking and cutting cost usually gives us more of the same and costs a lot more in the long run. Therefore "framing" is so important. The O.G. foundation goes deep, several stories deep. Deep enough to support skyscrapers. It would be unfortunate to only build a hut on this level of greatness. Building a home or community to "code" can result in you having at least the minimum allowable integrity. What happens when you allow outside standards to dictate your capabilities?

Code Enforcement

When you are building a home there are standards you will need to meet whether you like it or not. The fines and penalties for not meeting these standards are steep and will hamper completion of your project if they are not met. I used a reputable builder and my home was completed on time passing all inspections. Several months into living in my new house, I realized all the things I should have done during the building process. I realized the generally accepted building codes in many cases did not reflect my personal standards. It was not at O.G. - Obtaining Greatness level. I'm ashamed to say I built with the minimum in mind and not the best.

No one rises to low expectations. In some communities, people are treated like animals. The minimally expected behavior is so low that a reflection of greatness seems impossible. Standards should be set higher. Do you remember your elders telling you, you needed to be twice as good? Some of you know what I'm talking about. This level of work ethic allowed some of us to excel to great heights.

No one wants to live in a society that inflicts such harsh inequality, but when you "frame" this as the standard that you set for yourself, that's O.G - Obtaining Greatness. Only you can enforce "O.G. Code." This is the code that is of the highest quality and marksmanship. Everyone else's "code" will leave you living below your privilege, capabilities and keep you in your place without you realizing what's happening. It will give you perceived safety if you settle for your lot in life. Serving and protecting means you take the risk. When you take the risk, you also receive the reward. So, what can go wrong? The insulation value of different materials varies significantly and it is essential to know this throughout your construction project.

Walls, Doors and Windows

Your highest R-value will come from your walls. In the Old Testament, there was an O.G. named King Solomon. There was a young Shulamite woman who caught King Solomon's attention in the book, "The Song of Solomon." In the story this young woman is represented as a "Wall," meaning she had the highest respect for herself and was not "defiled" before marriage. This contrasts with being described as a door which has R-value (albeit less than a wall) when used appropriately but has the risk of having no value if it is carelessly left open.

Wall-mart

Whenever you attempt to be all things to everybody, you usually come up short. To be respected you must stand for something. Purchased respect will not protect you for very long because there will always be a higher bidder. Or in the opposite case, you will bid yourself out of business by selling out for the lowest price. You can't buy walls. They should be constructed; they must be layered to provide the promised R-value or in our community's case, respect. When you attempt to shortcut the process you short-circuit the protection. In our community any time you see someone on the news who has blown a fuse, nine times out of ten, it will not end well. Walls in our community allow respect and they also protect. Can you respect the position and the authority even if you don't like the person?

Open-door policy

When I was a kid, my mom would always get on me about holding the door open. She would say, "You're letting all these flies in." Or if it was wintertime, "You're letting all the heat out!" There is a talent drain in our community. As soon as we are able, and have the means to leave, we are out. Also, there is an influx of people who don't look like us that we allow in, only to see them drain our resources then take them back to their communities. Of course, we always want our children to go off and see the world, educate themselves, and become successful. We always pray they will come back and we would be able to provide them with success here at home. What role do you play in providing a home to come back to? Home meaning someplace with the opportunity to live and have a great family (not your basement). Would there be a greater desire to come back home where they grew up? Unlike the Shulamite woman, are we allowing any and everyone to come into us, our community? Why not prepare for our own?

To the window, to the wall

The ultimate protection comes from knowing who you are. When you know who you are, you're less likely to do stupid stuff. Also, you are less likely to project your junk onto others. Continuing with our materials analogy, we know the greatest R-value comes from the walls then a lesser value from the doors. What about the windows? Windows are unique because they are multi-functional. Unlike the walls where we calculate an R-value based upon heat resistance, windows use what's called a U-value which measures the conductivity of the glass. Very simply put, an R-value is the reciprocal of the U-value. The smaller the U-value the higher the R-value. So, what is "U?" U is you, or your ego. The smaller the ego, the higher the respect.

There are elements in other communities that are not consistent with an O.G. community. When you look out, what you see is mostly a reflection of what's inside of you. What you see is determined by what you are focusing on and what has your attention. When you protect your senses, they will protect you. What is your U-value? If it's too large, you just might find yourself doing whatever you are big and bad enough to do.

When I was a kid, I was "as nasty as they wanna be." If you aren't respected, then you will not be protected. Often, restraint is respected. Again, don't be so emotional. Just because you can doesn't mean you should. Remember, the generally accepted building code is not O.G. code. It's building to the minimum instead of the highest quality. Everyone speaks and acts before thinking. In your community keep your walls up, keep your windows clean and use your doors purposefully.

Hammertime (Can't touch this)

Now it is time to seal the deal. This can be your first or your last line of defense depending on the situation. We have talked a lot about knowing ourselves and leading our families. I can't stress enough the importance of understanding the long game. This helps you exercise the self-control needed to mount this defense. This defense is knowledge of the law. Knowledge of the law cannot come about only by spending time in the criminal justice system but also in civil court and with seeking expert opinion.

How tight are your contracts? There are some folks where a handshake just won't do. Having adequate legal representation must rank high on your list of priorities especially when it comes to doing business. Your attorney is an integral part of your team. I am going to challenge you to think like an O.G. Your mindset should shift from thinking you need an attorney because you are doing something wrong to I need an attorney because I am doing something right.

We want to establish more and better offense along with our well-established defense. I have met young brothers who are masters when it comes to the criminal justice system and the legal maneuvers they, or their loved ones, are taken through. They can tell you exactly how much time will be given for an offense based on the attorney, the judge, evidence and other circumstances. It really doesn't surprise me when a young brother who has been disadvantaged in certain areas exercises his God-given wisdom and talent within. We, the community, just need to change the arena and provide that young man a safe place to hone his skill set.

The same thing happens when the young man decides to leave the streets and go legit. He has more experience and insight than some C suite executives. It's usually the absence of legal advice that stunts his business or hinders his competitiveness. Your attorney works for you. Find someone you can trust and take the time to build a relationship. You do your heirs an excellent service by keeping all your legal affairs airtight from conception until it is passed to the next generation. Sometimes the pen is mightier than the sword and money spent on professionals is money well spent.

O.G. Code - Foot Soldiers

Establish the non-negotiable rules of your community. The police are already tough on crime and in many cases, overzealous. It works better if you get tough first. You must have a vested interest in something before you can protect it to the best of your abilities. This includes physical protection but just as relevant is the standard set, implemented and enforced internally. The strategic plan for your community calls for your boots on the ground. Where are my soldiers?

Come back to your community
Own your community
Police your community
Secure your community

It takes dedication and sacrifice to make a real difference. Ask yourself these questions:

• Do you owe your community?

- Is making a difference in your community worth being uncomfortable?
- Is your community worth more than your status and prestige?
- Do you see value in your community?
- Are you ready to take an "L" (loss) for your community?
- Are you willing to get your hands dirty?
- Are you prepared to stand up for your community?

Some so-called O.G.'s move out and never look back. It's easy to drink the integration Kool-Aid and lose your identity. If you found yourself answering "no" to a few of these questions, you might get your O.G. card revoked, if it was ever issued.

Conclusion

Maslow's hierarchy of needs lets us know next to food, water, and shelter; safety and security complete the foundation upon which everything else is built. A deep public policy discussion may be outside the scope of this book but it is needed. We must be at the table for that discussion to make our communities safe (with you leading). When a community is secure it's a lot easier for it to become prosperous. Sometimes we are prosperous and we don't even know it. This has a lot to do with how we define prosperity. The last chapter is the key that unlocks and reveals the destination of a real O.G. - Obtaining Greatness community.

Whatever we believe about ourselves
and our ability comes true for us.

–- Susan L. Taylor

Chapter XV - Wealth Management
The Prosperity Law
The goal is legacy

If everyone's not included, you are not prosperous. Develop a new vision of what prosperity looks like. It's a lot more than money. It should be inclusive.

Loose Change

You have a great life and you don't even know it. The fact you are still here, that you have made it to the end of this book, lets me know there is greatness in you. Greatness is in all of us. Most of the time it's just a slight adjustment or a minor tweak here and there, that aligns us with our purpose. Now a small misalignment, over time, can cause you to miss the mark entirely, but the change you need to go from good to great is not huge. The journey is not a straight shot. It winds and meanders through your territory as you see it and we hit our target through a lifetime of small adjustments. All your significant changes have already been addressed. We have discussed the microenvironment, now we'll end speaking to what this means to each one of you. You should answer this question, "What will be my legacy?"

The Prosperity Law is not about money. It's about longevity. Remember we talked about wealth being measured in time? You've heard the term generational wealth, but you can't call it wealth unless it spans more than a generation. Success is not success without a successor. One of the most significant concerns small business owners face when I advise them is succession planning. All your life you've counted every penny only to miss this million-dollar question of who takes over? What happens when I'm gone?

Money is just a metaphor I'm using. It could be your health, it could be inadequate estate planning, or just a dummy move made in haste. Closing those loose ends that threaten your legacy is important. Jesus said in the book Song of Solomon 2:15, "It's the small foxes that spoil the vine." We started this book focused on "you," and no matter how large "you" become, we still need to attend to the details. Those small details can threaten your legacy. The big stuff, we can see it coming. Finding value in the seemingly insignificant will make the difference. Those dimes, nickels, and pennies we start overlooking will eventually become dollars. They were significant all along. Likewise, we can't wait until our life is used up to realize the priceless moments that should have been poured into someone so our legacy continues. What does this mean when it comes to our community?

Deep in the money

You must see the intrinsic value of each one, individually, and in groups collectively. This value can be assessed on the surface or read in a blueprint. Meaning it can be visible or will need to be deciphered. As you recognize value, what do you do with it? An O.G.'s focus is always on adding value, but don't allow yourself to forget you have added value over time. If you ignore the amount you have added in the past, situations can arise, and you lose sight of your personal worth, or you won't recognize new opportunities.

The option for greatness won't be exercised or executed on time. God puts it in front of you but exercising the option, in this case, is not automatic. However, should you decide to implement, God is obligated to deliver. In His heavenly clearinghouse, no transaction goes unfulfilled. There is no counter party risk. He will do what he said. But, you do have free will. So, it's your choice if some of your options expire worthless because you didn't recognize the value when it was there. God works through people.

When I recognized the call God placed on my life, I realized I had a right to everything stated in my contract with Him and He had an obligation to deliver. I had a right to live an abundant life. I am a prosperity preacher, but the Prosperity Law I preach and teach focuses on the community. Get yourself right, get your family right then get your community right.

With the help of your Creator and putting Him first you can accomplish this, and I promise you, the money will be a byproduct. When we're focused on the money first we are out of order. The calling is reduced to just your gift that you are attempting to exploit. This is the difference between being talented and being anointed. Always recognize the value in the people God has called you unto.

Covered Calls

Prosperity is living your life according to God's plan and His will for your life. You will have times when you are "called out," meaning an event will trigger in your life where you must exercise your faith. The outcome you want is already yours! As an O.G. you understand God has you covered and any triggering event you will be compensated for.

With the Prosperity Law you are owning this call. You recognize the environment you are operating in. You are in tune at a level where you know the premium placed on your life will sustain you in hard times. You know you'll be compensated for anything God requires you to give up. In God's economy, even in tough times, He will protect you, if you put it in His hands.

Again, God works through people (I can't say this enough). We talked about trust and this will surface throughout your journey. We need each other and prosperity does not fly solo. If you have developed the mindset that it's lonely at the top, that's not the O.G. -

Obtaining Greatness mindset. It's lonely at the top because you out ran everyone. With that said, is this your final destination? That is not prosperity. How are you the only one prosperous? There are some things you can do on your own. If you're in your F-22 fighter jet always looking for trouble, you should remember something. It only seats one and you have a higher probability of getting shot down sooner or later. Prosperity is that A380 where the community is thriving. Some people don't believe this is possible. I think if you get the right people in the right seats on this plane, piloted by competent leadership, we will arrive at our destination. Don't let the turbulence scare you. Yes, it takes vision, but don't underestimate the tools at your disposal. The best, most sophisticated, and meticulously designed tools.

The World's Finest Chocolate

You have a purpose. You are a tool in the hands of God as he cultivates and prepares this O.G. - Obtaining Greatness generation. Understand your purpose allows you to align with the Prosperity Law. My mission is to create, teach and implement economic tools and strategies to help people change their lives and, leave a positive legacy. Leaving a positive legacy is essential for families and has been prioritized in many communities. The importance the black woman plays, and has played for many generations, has never been so evident to me. Not only in her (our) community, but also in wealthy white communities she has been significant.

When I worked in wealth management, I assisted high net-worth clients with their investment decisions. These are not the type of relationships which are built overnight but over time. You get to know your clients on a very intimate basis. Most of them were hard-working and industrious, pulling themselves up by their bootstraps types. There were others who inherited their wealth or remember a relatively carefree lifestyle made possible by their family wealth. My career was a learning experience far beyond my formal education. I found myself in a very unique position.

Many clients who inherited their wealth and had the proverbial silver-spoon, were raised with black nannies or, "The help," as they were called. This allowed white men and women to go about securing their legacy and building wealth. We must give credit where credit is due. Those children were nurtured and provided for, and loved by black women. This did just as much to secure those children's future, as did their inheritances. As a man, now as I see these elderly women in the community, at church, or listen to the stories of family and friends, I have a new-found respect for the contributions and wealth creation from black women.

Finer Womanhood

Black women have for generations supported their community, their children and their men. As a black man, my power is enhanced when I know I have a black woman behind me. In our patriarchal society the roles of women, and especially black women, have been ignored throughout history. The strength of black women has only recently been acknowledged in the mainstream. This has been in large part because of the perceived absence of black men leading their households and communities. Bold, beautiful, and courageous, black women have stood in the gap for black men as we've struggled with various issues directly and indirectly.

The love of God flows through her heart with a level of compassion we all should model. "Who can find a virtuous woman?" the scripture says. I see them every day planting and harvesting from the ground fertilized with the sweat of her brow, and the watering of her tears. I see them nursing humanity and providing strength and nourishment. Even if she didn't birth naturally she has birthed spiritually on every level. I see them in corporate America holding it down nine to five, coming home and mothering from six to ten, and loving her man from 11 until.

O.G., there is no greatness without the black woman. She is to be cherished and revered. It's one of those unspoken truths. If we look at history, even the ugliest part of it, we see her value. "It is far above rubies" and "strength and honor are her clothing." O.G. - Obtaining Greatness, men and women, we acknowledge this and never drop our energies below this level of respect. Protecting, respecting and uplifting our black women (all women) must be in our DNA.

B.A.P.'s

The Prosperity Law shines all over Black women. The beauty, ingenuity, and grit persevere over the tallest obstacles. Her very nature and essence speak of strength over time. That sounds like an O.G. if I've ever heard of one. Prosperity is about wholeness, but it does include fundraising. Proverbs chapter 31:15-16 speaks of her ability to influence her household financially. Since slavery, black women have played an integral part in sustaining their family alongside black men.

When I was a kid, our school would sell chocolate bars to raise money for our field trips. Unfortunately, sometimes I ate more chocolate than I sold. This caused me to come up short even though it was designed for my profit. Men, you cannot afford to misuse our black women. Not only will you come up short but you rob her of her purpose in your life as a helpmate.

All a man's success and achievement can be attributed to having the right woman by his side. She is your "Why." She is to be treasured, honored and esteemed above all else, less God. She is your queen. This is the most powerful piece in our prosperity. We are raising Black American Princesses. Our daughters need to see how they are to be treated. Men, you are more than just a "black man in America." You are a king and black women have treated us as such. If you disagree then change your focus. The book of Philippians chapter 4:8 tells us how. Men, hold on to your black women. She is the finest and you are a fool to let her get away.

American Pharaoh

O.G., you are a king! I challenge you to win within. I challenge you to win at home. I challenge you to win in your community. With the help of your black queen by your side you can win all three races. Your faith is strengthened by the years of preparation. You are there for your family providing leadership and stability. Now, you are saving your community by showing up and serving.

O.G., you are the substance of things hoped for and the evidence of things not seen. How long have you lived beneath your privilege and relinquished your kingship to those less deserving? The Prosperity Law is the law of faith as well as legacy. Even in your darkest hour you must believe. You must believe and teach your children to believe. Your belief becomes a part of your very being and, for better or worse, your children's. There's a quote attributed to the industrialist Henry Ford that says, "If you think you can or think you can't, either way, you are right." This is a critical tool when building your legacy.

Throughout history we see questionable men rise to the heights of achievement because they <u>believed</u> that they could. Also, we see men with royalty in their veins diminished to almost nothing because they thought that they could not. O.G. faith can, O.G. faith does. At this point in your life, O.G. faith has completed what others said could not be done. You believed you could make it, you persevered and got the job done. Here you are still standing after all that life has thrown at you. This is what prosperity looks like.

Train up a child in the way that he should go and when he is old he will not depart from it. *Ps 22:6*

It is a beautiful thing to see an O.G.'s family. A family where everyone is on one accord teaching and living by the principles presented here in this book. I celebrate you O.G. because lesser men would have died in the struggle. Lesser men would have gotten offended and exhausted their energy arguing. Yes, some men will not reach O.G. Status, but even that does not stop the O.G. from reaching out by being a father to the fatherless or a brother to his friend in need. Your family is broad and includes children you may not have given seed to naturally, but by spiritual adoption you have made them your own. This is what prosperity looks like.

But thou shalt remember the LORD thy God: for it is he that giveth thee power to get wealth, that he may establish his covenant which he sware unto thy fathers, as it is this day. *Duet 8:18*

O.G., you are a businessman. This builds healthy communities and secures your legacy. Your legacy plus the legacies of many others is what creates sustainable, thriving communities. You understand the value of the dollars that circulate in your community. You were built for this, and as the insights from past preparation kicks in, you rise to heights not knowing how you did it. But, you do know how you did it. God has given you the power to get wealth meaning He has given you time. This was the last race to secure your legacy in the history of great achievers. You exercised your faith, you took care of your family, and you financed your community. You made it! This is what prosperity looks like.

Now that you have made it don't judge others, but understand the conditions that kept them from making it. Some common reasons include inequality and lack of opportunity. What I found to be a significant hindrance to the O.G. mindset is offense or being offended. When you are maimed by an offense, you lose your legs, and you can't run as fast. Many times, someone must carry you. You could be put out to pasture or worse. Whatever the reason why, you are too slow. You may have the same amount of time as me, but I'm covering way more ground than you are because I let some stuff go. I'm not going to tell you don't get offended because then you must believe that it is possible to do.

You are justified by faith. It doesn't matter what you've been through or, what you're still in! You are a winner. When you are a winner, how much more valuable is your seed? If you are a complainer, your children will be complainers. An O.G. understands this and he guards his heart and mind against any foreign doctrine that causes him to lose. Energy expounded to offense must be transferred to awakening the O.G. within. Yes, it's already in you, but you must believe it. When you are awakened to how powerful you are, the hard work and effort do not seem as bad. In fact, you will eagerly anticipate putting in the work every day. You must believe this brother! If you don't believe it you won't do it.

Horse Shoes

Opportunity is missed by most people because it is dressed in overalls and looks like work
—*Thomas A. Edison*

264

The O.G. - Obtaining Greatness mindset is hard work. Not just hard mental work, but get down and dirty manual labor hard work. You will never win a race if you are too lazy to lace up your boots. Now, I understand the work smart instead of a hard crowd. You should be careful though of someone who puts work into avoiding hard work. I heard an old man say once, "That dog won't hunt." You might not know that until you're in the field. At that time, it is too late because it is time to perform. You will not receive an O.G. performance from someone who does not like to work hard. Hard work is therapeutic for your mind and body.

The physiological effects of strenuous movement release endorphins in your brain that put you in a better mood. This is why working out at the gym is important. Hard work is the prerequisite to winning any race. None of what we discussed in the previous chapters just happens. You must work for it. People who work at the O.G. mindset appear lucky to the people who will not. "The harder I work, the luckier I become." This quote was attributed to Thomas Jefferson. O.G.! It's your time! Polish those shoes and get busy. But, only if you are willing to strap on those boots and get busy. This, too, is what prosperity looks like and it leads to another vital area that will cement your legacy in an O.G. community, service.

Indentured Servants

An O.G. community is filled with people who believe they owe a debt to the community and they are proud to fulfill it. Who doesn't like paying their bills? O.G. 101, integrity taught us this a long time ago. The integrity of our community is bound together with the gifts, talents, and abilities shared and offered. This includes money, if you are wondering. An O.G. doesn't question. He gets the job done. There is always plenty of money if the investment returns are there. You do need labors though. This is a labor of love for the community. You are not trying to purchase your freedom, but you are securing your legacy with your blood, sweat, and tears. This is the only way a legacy is built. I encourage you to love the skin you're in, but expand upon that idea. You should love the community you're in. You are working for your children's future. You care about your children, right?

People do not care how much you know until they know how much you care. - *John Maxwell*

One of the challenges faced in the Wealth Management industry happens when client's offspring lose the incentive to work. The "struggle" is hard to pass down, or inherit. It's what made us who we are today. On one hand, you work hard to keep your children from going through what you went through. On the other, you're stopping them from having access to what made you the O.G. you have grown to be. Just remember, you control the thermostat. Here are some suggestions to keep your seeds in growth mode as you nurture them.

1. Practice restraint as a parent.

When we were poor the T.V. was the babysitter. Now, you think you can be let off the parenting hook for a few extra dollars and personal freedoms. Unfortunately by practicing restraint, you become the oddball parent living in the dark ages, relative to their friends. Don't give in; this is not a place to cave for convenience.

2. Challenge your children.

Tie vacations and extracurricular activities to goals achieved.

Teach them to create S.M.A.R.T.O.G. goals. This is more difficult for the parent. They will appreciate something to strive for and the sense of accomplishment when the goal is reached.

3. Make them volunteer.

This is what most schools do now. It develops a sense of responsibility and service. Consider spending part of your holiday serving at a homeless shelter or food pantry.

4. Tailor your estate plan and share with them.

There will be "X" amount of dollars at different intervals and milestones. Provide a match to their salaries for an incentive.

5. Make practical decisions

Concerning college, weddings and first home down payments, make sure it's feasible. Talk about these decisions and try not to raise expectations too high. Their level of maturity will determine how much cash you shower on them at any time.

Whatever you do, don't take away their desire to serve. This selfless trait is becoming more difficult to come by in this younger generation. Legacy seems like something far removed in the future to young people. Wealth management is time management. Find time to serve together. They need to see you so they understand what legacy and prosperity look like.

40 Acres of Diamonds

Thinking we can have prosperity without serving causes us to (like in chapter one) orbit in this community sized holding pattern. We will not be cleared to land with this thinking, and for the most part, it is self-imposed. No one is coming to save us and no one's giving back what was stolen, not without a revolution. If they did give it back, it would change hands again within a generation or two if these laws aren't implemented.

For the weapons of our warfare are not carnal, but mighty through God to the pulling down of strongholds. *2 Corinthians 10:4*

So how do we optimize our time? How do we manage our wealth? Start by recognizing and managing the resources in your hand. Your community is valuable, and as you are chasing land in other communities, someone else is picking your pocket for yours. Why is that? Because it has value. Stop coveting and start cultivating, excavating and building. Develop the land and your people.

In 1911, a scholar named Elder Watson Diggs, on the campus of Indiana University Bloomington founded an organization of men who were dedicated to "achievement in every area of human endeavor." This organization has since built hundreds of thousands of men on the campuses of various universities around the world. He is not here to see the fruit of his labor, but men around the world are thankful for his leadership and insight that gave us a code to live by based on achievement.

These are the men we need in our community. A great incentive is the expansion of the central business districts (downtowns) many of our communities border against if not encompassing them entirely. We are sitting on our "Acres of Diamonds," but we continue to sell the farm in search of fake greener pastures.

When I was a kid, I worked at the neighborhood grocery store that was owned by a family friend, Ed Benson. Ed was like a father to many young kids in the neighborhood and provided many jobs to youth in the community. This is relevant as we close because the store's slogan and jingle was, "Don't ask if we have it, ask where it is." When you look at your community, and have a difficult time seeing the value, don't leave and go somewhere else. I challenge you to "Don't ask if we have it, ask where it is." Don't assume we can't but ask how can we? You internalized the O.G. - Obtaining Greatness mindset. Your community is internalizing you and me to build wealth and leave a positive legacy. It's up to you, O.G., what prosperity will look like in our communities.

O.G. Code - Estate Plan

Your first job as a citizen of the O.G. community is financial planning. We need you to dissimulate this information so The Prosperity Law will operate in our community. These documents must be executed as an O.G. These are your legacy documents.

- I-Will. - Make a commitment to leave a legacy in your community. An O.G.'s resolve cannot be contested. When you do this, your gift will pass unencumbered to your offspring. This can be the offspring of both your natural and spiritual seed.
- Term, life - This is a lifetime commitment. While it seems like a lot, this is a small price relative to the benefit gained by the beneficiaries. Their lives will never be the same.
- Trust - When we build trust in our community it becomes an entity of its own. Trust provides protection from people who take advantage of us. Spell it out and let it be known how your community will operate.
- Real estate plan - You are builders by nature. Buy back the block, keep the title and deed restrict. Self-gentrify.

- Social Security - Develop the mindset "everybody eats." You are your brother's keeper. Never allow yourself to be satisfied if someone is hungry. There's enough for everybody.
- Pension - No one will take care of you and your community but you. Loyalty to someone else's system will not get you a check. Become the check signer instead of just being a check casher.
- Long-term care - Memory loss can take everything you've learned here. Write the vision! Make sure you develop the O.G. - Obtaining Greatness mindset. Whenever you hear "O.G.," think of what you have read in this book. Change your mindset, change your life.

Conclusion

Have you ever looked up at the stars and imagined traveling through space? Or, what about uploading your consciousness into a computer? I know, it sounds like something from a Sci-Fi movie or comic book. The same could be said about the cell phone in your purse or pocket about 35 years ago. Think about it. Imagine it's the year 1983. The cell phone you had then was used for talking only and cost approximately $4,000.00 (about $8,000.00 priced for inflation). Now, think of all the devices replaced and the increased functionality of today's cell phone. It would be hard to imagine something that was once a luxury would become so commonplace. There were people who, even in 1983, could imagine the devices we use now. They could in their imaginations visualize the future. Their meta-cognition was on a different level than everyone else. This is where we get some of the artificial intelligence or A.I. methodology we have today. You must look at how you think. It's the only way to break out of an old mindset.

Are the futuristic thought leaders of yesterday and today so much different from you and I physiologically? Do you have far more information and capabilities than what was available to you 30 years ago? In the age of free information, you can't allow the opportunity to escape. In this age of big data, you can't afford to think with old mindsets. You run the risk of falling back into slavery if you were ever free. This O.G. mindset must be injected into "OUR" children. I stress "our" because of the emphasis placed on science, technology, engineering and math (S.T.E.M.) in other cultures. We finally wised up and brought back the arts (S.T.E.A.M.). What makes this even more potent for the O.G. is adding entrepreneurship (E.S.T.E.A.M.). Put entrepreneurship first so that it's always an option. Believe this with your whole heart.

You are more than enough to accomplish everything we have discussed in these pages. I believe changing your mindset is critical to your survival. Some forces would love to eliminate you and your offspring. This is not hyperbole. If you think I'm exaggerating, look at the nationalist mindset. It's not sweeping the country. It's coming out of the shadows. There is no fear, or hate, in the O.G. - Obtaining Greatness way. You are better than that. You can't afford to keep old mindsets. Your legacy depends on it.

"The mind, once stretched by a new idea, never returns to its original dimensions."

— *Ralph Waldo Emerson*

"When you control a man's thinking you do not have to worry about his actions."

— *Carter G. Woodson*

Epilogue - The Next Generation

The O.G. - Obtaining Greatness mindset is all about the long game. Will you be around to see it? Maybe, or maybe not. At least plant your seeds so you give your children a chance to eat. They can eat what they produce. They will know how to produce. Prophesy to your seed, both natural and spiritual, what you want to see come to pass. If you've ever attended a black church revival, you may appreciate this story.

I attended a revival at my church, and I was excited to receive a word from God. The music was loud, and the spirit was high. With each increasing chord progression struck on the organ, praise would erupt from the congregation. This revival was unique in that two female evangelists were ministering. One evangelist would minister through the spoken word, and the other would minister through song. They did this as the "Spirit" lead them.

Now at that time, I was a single father of three children; my son Andre Jr. and his two older sisters Arielle and Andrea. They attended this church service with me. Toward the end of the service, there was a shift to the prophetic part of ministering where a specific (or general) "word" from God through his messenger/minister is delivered to an individual. I had already gone to the altar for a group altar call. As I stood there, the evangelist came and stood right in front of me. She looked at me, and told me to close my eyes, and to raise my hands. I closed my eyes and lifted my hands. Then I heard her speak.

"The Spirit of the Lord is showing me your leadership ability."
I don't get overly excited in these instances, I guess because I've been in church most of my life.

"There is something in your future that has to do with business."

In my heart, I was receiving what she was saying and in total agreement. She continued.

"Don't worry about the resources or how you're going to do it just know that thou God see'th thee! God is bringing you confirmation in this hour."

I still had my eyes closed and the organist, along with the rest of the band, was on fire! With the music so loud and with my eyes closed, it was hard to sense the proximity of the evangelist. She continued.

"I see you influencing many people and your words will travel the nations. You are a chosen vessel for your generation."

She continued, but at this point I wasn't "in the spirit" as much as I should have been. Now I'm tempted to peek one eye open to see what's going on around me. So, I took a look. I could hear her voice still loud and clear, but I didn't see her. I opened both eyes. There where at least a few dozen people close together with their arms raised, and I didn't want to be too evident in looking for this woman.

"What you need has already been planted deep inside you and in due season it shall spring forth!"

Yes, she had moved away from me and had moved on. This action was confusing because her prophetic words seamlessly rolled as if she was telling me a story. When my eyes found her, about twenty feet away, she was still flowing with the same prophetic word:

"...and as you allow God to use you a greater harvest shall come into your life..."

This woman of God was giving MY prophecy to someone else! But upon closer inspection, seeing through the raised arms and exuberant worship, I recognized who she was now speaking to. She was talking to my son, Andre Jr!

"...and the fear and disobedience that has held back previous generations will not hold back this Joshua generation. Believe and receive what thus saith the Lord!"

It wasn't what she said but how she delivered the message. It made me better understand succession and legacy and the multi-generational nature of God's blessing. We serve an infinite God! I didn't fully understand until I wrote this book. That was the O.G. - Obtaining Greatness mindset. Don't expect to accomplish everything you envision personally. The vision should always be more substantial than you, more significant than your family even. Ecclesiastics 3:11 says, "He has made everything beautiful in its time. Also, He has put eternity in their hearts, except that no one can find out the work that God does from beginning to end."

It's always more abundant than you O.G.! That's one way to tell if you're on the right path. Ask yourself the question, "Is this too big to do on my own?" If the answer is yes, then I say, go for it!

ACKNOWLEDGEMENTS

I'm grateful to the many people who made *O.G. - Obtaining Greatness* possible, starting with my wonderful family:

To my wife Traci, thank you for always believing in me, supporting me and being a wonderful mother to our children.

To my daughter Andrea, thank you for loving me past my mistakes and giving me peace of mind as a parent.

To my daughter Arielle, thank you for your giving heart and spirit to serve. You are a daddy's girl.

To my son Andre, Jr., thank you for your strength of character, your humor, artistic gifts and creativity. I live vicariously through you.

To my uncle Jerome, thank you for being a father when you didn't have to be. You have the heart of a lion.

To my mother Sheila Ray, thank you for your open arms of acceptance and encouragement. You loved me regardless of the circumstances.

To my parents, Nate and Gerceda Guinn, thank you for your model of marriage and family and allowing me to be your son.

To my siblings, cousins, Aunts, Uncles, extended family and friends, thank you for keeping me grounded and providing me a wonderful childhood with great memories.

I would also like to thank my mentor and fraternity brother

Jimmy E. Greene. Your offense provided a great hole for me to run through. The SVAALTI brotherhood/sisterhood will be a great jewel in your legacy. This is only the beginning.

I want to thank my Victorious Believers Ministries church family for their continuous support through the years. You are my friends. The Pryor legacy is an important part of my foundation and I'm forever grateful.

Thank you to my wonderful readers and social media followers. You give me the opportunity to share my thoughts and I'm enriched by our dialogue and discussion. To all the thought leaders keeping positive black life front and center, I appreciate you and offer encouragement. We do it for the culture. Let's elevate, let's be great!

In loving memory,
Clara B. Smith
James and Ethel Pierrie
Elma Harris

Rae-Lynn Buckley
I remember what you told me.

BOOK NOW!

As a motivational speaker, Andre L. Buckley's success story of sacrifice, hard work, and perseverance as well as the powerful and poetic way he communicates it, will inspire any audience. Much more than a financial advisor, Andre shares his unique growth strategies, which will empower audience members to make positive changes in every aspect of their lives for immediate and long-term success. Andre L. Buckley, will reveal how you too can live the Dream, American or otherwise.

www.andrebuckley.com/speak.

CPSIA information can be obtained
at www.ICGtesting.com
Printed in the USA
LVHW081008041019
633199LV00013B/170/P